Attention Deficit / Hyperactivity Disorder

of related interest

From Thoughts to Obsessions
Obsessive Compulsive Disorder in Children and Adults
Per Hove Thomsen
ISBN 1 85302 721 9 pb

Asperger's Syndrome
A Guide for Parents and Professionals
Tony Attwood
ISBN 1 85302 577 1 pb

Through the Eyes of Aliens
A Book about Autistic People
Jasmine Lee O' Neill
ISBN 1 85302 710 3 pb

Children with Autism 2nd Edition
Diagnosis and Interventions to Meet their Needs
Colwyn Trevarthen, Kenneth Aitken, Despina Papoudi and Jacqueline Robarts
ISBN 1 85302 555 0 pb

Attention Deficit / Hyperactivity Disorder
A Multidisciplinary Approach

Henryk Holowenko

Jessica Kingsley Publishers
London and Philadelphia

The right of Henryk Holowenko to be identified as author of this work has been asserted by him in accordance with the Copyright, Designs and Patents Act 1988.

First published in the United Kingdom in 1999 by

Jessica Kingsley Publishers Ltd,
116 Pentonville Road,
London N1 9JB, England

and

325 Chestnut Street,
Philadelphia PA 19106, USA.

www.jkp.com

© Copyright 1999 Henryk Holowenko

Library of Congress Cataloging in Publication Data
A CIP catalog record for this book is available from the Library of Congress

British Library Cataloguing in Publication Data
A CIP catalog record for this book is available from the British Library

ISBN 1 85302 741 3 pb

Printed and Bound in Great Britain by
Athenaeum Press, Gateshead, Tyne and Wear

There is a normal type of character, for example, in which impulses seem to discharge so promptly into movements that inhibitions get no time to arise. These are the 'dare-devil' and 'mercurial' temperaments, overflowing with animation, and fizzling with talk...

William James (1890, p.800) *Principles of Psychology*

Contents

FOREWORD AND ACKNOWLEDGEMENTS 9

1. Introduction 11

2. Outline and General Issues 13

   Background 13
   Definition: What is AD/HD? 14
   Causes / Etiology 15
   Comorbidities and Associated Problems 17
   Why is AD/HD Difficult to Diagnose? 18
   Overview of AD/HD 20

3. Diagnosis and Assessment Considerations 23

   Developmental and Family History 25
   Behaviour Across Settings 25
   Review of School/Preschool Records 26
   Individual Psychological Assessment
   and Cognitive Profile 27
   Clinical and Medical Examination 30
   Integrating Assessment Data 31

4. Interventions at School 33

   School Based Strategies and Interventions for
   Children Diagnosed as Having AD/HD 33
   Classroom Management 34
   Home and School 41
   Summary 42

5. Interventions at Home   45

    Develop Knowledge and Understanding   46
    Think and Act Positively About your Child   46
    Develop a Positive Self-Esteem for your Child   47
    Implement Routine, Structure and Predictability   48
    Communicate Clearly   49
    Take Control   49
    Have Realistic Expectations   50
    Set up Sanctions ('Safety Valves')   50
    Take Care of Yourself   52
    Seek Advice   52

6. Medication   53

    Side Effects   54
    Addiction   54
    The Treatment Decision   55
    Follow-Up   55

7. Educational Provision: AD/HD and the   57
    SEN Code of Practice

8. Parents and the Assessment and Intervention   61
    Process

9. Policy Guidelines   65

    APPENDIX A: DIAGNOSTIC CRITERIA   71
        DSM-IV DIAGNOSTIC CRITERIA FOR AD/HD   71
        ICD-10 DIAGNOSTIC CRITERIA FOR   74
        HYPERKINETIC SYNDROME
    APPENDIX B: PHYSICIAN'S CHECKLIST FOR PATIENTS   77
    APPENDIX C: AD/HD INFORMATION SHEET   83
    FOR PARENTS
        SUGGESTIONS FOR KEEPING YOUR CHILD SAFE   83
        TAKING YOUR CHILD OUT TO A PUBLIC PLACE   84
    REFERENCES   87
    FURTHER READING   93
    FURTHER INFORMATION AND CONTACT ADDRESSES   97
    SUBJECT INDEX   101
    AUTHOR INDEX   107

Foreword and Acknowledgements

This book has been written following consultation with a cross-county multidisciplinary working group which met in Devon between December 1996 and June 1997, and has subsequently been updated to reflect current research and practice. It represents as far as possible a consensus view within the working group on the disparate positions held about AD/HD in the literature and amongst professional practices. The multidisciplinary composition of the group reflects the need to facilitate a multi-modal collaborative approach in the assessment and intervention process which involves parents, teachers, psychologists and medical practitioners. The working group involved:

Henryk Holowenko
(Chair) Educational Psychologist – East Devon

Dr Tony Cronin
Consultant Paediatrician – West Devon

Mollie Curry
Advisory Teacher: Behaviour Support Team – East Devon

Dr Rosemary Evans
Consultant Community Paediatrician – West Devon

Ken Fuller
Educational Psychologist – North Devon

Richard Haydon
Assistant Area Education Officer – North Devon

Wolfgang Hug
Adviser for SEN – Devon

Dr Yvette Parker
Consultant Child Psychiatrist – East Devon

Jackie Pile
AD/HD Wise – South Devon

Andy Simpson
Advisory Teacher: Behaviour Support Team – South Devon

Belinda Woodthorpe
Educational Psychologist – West Devon

Dr Rini Hoogkamer (Co-option)
Specialist Registrar in Child Psychiatry – East Devon

With special thanks to Nick Knapman (Deputy Principal Psychologist), Professor Martin Herbert (Clinical Psychologist), Jenny Wookey (Clinical Psychologist) and Geoffrey Kewley (Consultant Paediatrician) for their valuable suggestions and contributions.

CHAPTER I

Introduction

Today Attention Deficit / Hyperactivity Disorder (AD/HD) constitutes the most common childhood referral to psychiatric and psychological services in the United States and is subject to increasing public awareness, scrutiny and no small controversy in the UK and other countries. It is conservatively estimated to occur in 3 per cent to 6 per cent of children from diverse cultures and geographical regions, with an overrepresentation of boys by approximately 3:1 and encompasses the whole life-span, albeit with age and gender-related changes in its manifestations (Tannock 1998). There are huge discrepancies in reported incidence rates with up to 9 per cent of American children being diagnosed as AD/HD in certain regions of the USA compared to only 1 in 1500 in the UK (Hinshaw 1994; Prendergast *et. al.* 1988; Schachar 1991; Taylor 1994a; Taylor *et. al.* 1991). Kewley (1998) suggests that the condition is underdiagnosed and undertreated in Britain and reports data showing that approximately 0.03 per cent of schoolchildren are treated with psychostimulants in the UK compared with 1 per cent in Australia and 3 per cent in the USA.

Part of this discrepancy is due to different diagnostic criteria that are used in different countries to define the type of disorder (see Appendix A). However, even accounting for these and given estimations that 0.5 to 1 per cent of UK children have hyperkinesis (Taylor 1995), it seems likely that AD/HD has been significantly underdiagnosed and undertreated here.

With more children now being identified with AD/HD it has become increasingly important for teachers and other professionals working with these children to acquaint themselves with the nature of this condition. Furthermore, there is a need for a multi-modal collaborative approach to the assessment and intervention process – one which involves parents, teachers, psychologist and medical practitioner working together. If the relationships that form the core of the assessment and intervention process are strained, hostile and ill-formed, the entire assessment and intervention process will suffer – and ultimately the needs of the child as well.

This book has been written in order to provide guidelines for teachers, parents and other professionals on good practice in assessment, diagnosis, management and provision for children with AD/HD. The guidelines stress the need for a collaborative approach in relation to dealing with AD/HD. It is not intended to provide a detailed description of what is essentially an evolving concept (cf. British Psychological Society 1996) and, for some, a highly contentious issue. More detailed descriptions and discussions can be found in the references contained at the end of the book.

CHAPTER 2

Outline and General Issues

Background

Other than the name itself, there is nothing new about AD/HD. As is seen in the opening quotation, William James, who is regarded by many as the father of modern psychology, made reference to its symptoms in his *Principles of Psychology* over 100 years ago.

The medical record on AD/HD is said to have begun in 1902, when British paediatrician George Still published an account of 20 children in his practice who were 'passionate', defiant, spiteful and lacking 'inhibitory volition'. Still made the then radical suggestion that bad parenting was not to blame. Instead, he suspected a subtle brain injury. This theory gained greater credence in the years following the 1917–18 epidemic of viral encephalitis, when doctors observed that the infection left some children with impaired attention, memory and control over their impulses. In the 1940s and 1950s, and following studies of soldiers who had sustained head injuries in World War II, the same constellation of symptoms was called Minimal Brain Damage and later Minimal Brain Dysfunction. In 1937 an American paediatrician (Bradley) reported that giving stimulants to children with these symptoms had the unexpected effect of calming them down. By the mid-1970s, methylphenidate (Ritalin) had become the most prescribed drug for what was termed Attentional Deficit Disorder (ADD) and then eventually Attentional Deficit / Hyperactivity Disorder (AD/HD).

In our lifetime it is likely that the diagnostic label will change again. There are many who argue for example that we should call this condition Behavioural Inhibition Disorder (BID) since it is the lack of inhibitory control which appears to be at the core of the problem (Barkley 1996). We need to understand that the label is determined by a committee and a political process. The behaviours themselves, however, are very real and have consistently affected children in all cultures, throughout history – children, adolescents and adults of all ages.

Definition: What is AD/HD?

Attention Deficit / Hyperactivity Disorder (AD/HD) is a *behavioural* diagnosis of a medical condition which refers to a mixed group of disruptive behaviours. These behaviours can have many causes and effects and their characteristics merge with normal behaviour. AD/HD is a medical diagnostic label given when these behaviours cause difficulty with the child's:

- ° development
- ° behaviour and performance
- ° family relationships
- ° social interaction.

AD/HD has three main hallmarks: inattentiveness, an almost reckless impulsiveness and, in some but not all cases, a knee-jiggling, toe-tapping hyperactivity. Without hyperactivity, the disorder is called AD/HD-Inattentive Type. Such children have difficulty paying attention, sitting still, controlling their emotions and thinking about what they are going to do before they do it. They can be fearless and accident prone, have difficulty waiting their turn, blurt out answers in class, fail to follow rules and have difficulty staying on task. Because of their impulsive and frequently inattentive behaviour they are also at great risk socially and have difficulties forming relationships.

It is important to understand that what is being talked about here in these behaviours could actually be an exaggeration of what is age-appropriate behaviour. All children at different stages of development may experience problems acting impulsively, or have difficulty paying attention, or have problems sitting still; but it is a clustering of a group of these problems together, the intensity with which they occur, and their persistence across the child's development that is critical in identifying what is essentially a syndrome in childhood as AD/HD. Furthermore, symptoms of AD/HD can be the result of other factors, such as frustration with difficult schoolwork, lack of motivation, emotional concerns, or other medical conditions. It is not an all or nothing phenomenon. To make a careful diagnosis one must eliminate other explanations for the symptoms.

The goal is not simply to arrive at a diagnosis of AD/HD, but to determine an intervention plan that is likely to succeed, based on the information gathered.

For some with severe symptoms, medical treatment is critical to the child's ability to be able to function at school. However, it is important to recognise that pills are not a substitute for skills, and teaching strategies for management of the social or behavioural problems these children often exhibit is essential. The degree to which AD/HD is a handicap depends not only on the severity of the symptoms, but also on the environment. The right school or home situation can make all the difference.

Causes / Etiology

Research evidence regarding the causes of AD/HD remains inconclusive. Nevertheless, there is growing consensus that some kind of neurological and/or biochemical processes may be involved. Neurotransmitters involving dopamine, serotonin and noradrenalin have all been implicated as essential components for effective attention and impulse control. Studies using brain imaging techniques point to some consistent evidence of hemisphere dysfunction implicating the fronto-striatal networks in children with AD/HD (Castellanos *et al.* 1996; Giedd *et al.* 1996; Hauser *et al.* 1993; Zametkin *et al.* 1990).

There is also growing evidence of a strong genetic basis for the neurodysfunction seen in AD/HD. Twin studies show that genetic effects have been found to account for about half of the variance in measures of hyperactivity and inattentiveness (Van der Oord, Boomsma and Verhulst 1994; Goodman and Stevenson 1989; Sherman, McGue and Iacono 1997).

Other hypotheses to account for these variations in brain functioning range from inherited genetic characteristics, individual differences in normal variation, delay in neurological maturation, prenatal and postnatal insult, the effects of lead poisoning and medical treatment through to environmental aspects implicating contemporary culture or features of parent–child interactions (British Psychological Society 1996). In contrast to the weak evidence for environmental *causes* of AD/HD there is growing evidence supporting the impact of environmental factors upon the *course* and ultimate *outcome* of AD/HD (Kendall and Braswell 1985; Sonuga-Barke and Goldfoot 1995; Taylor and Dowdney 1998; Van der Oord and Rowe 1997).

Above all it is important to recognise that biological factors only predispose children to behave in certain ways and that biology is not destiny in this regard. One of the most important things in managing AD/HD is the taking of a broad view of the child's abilities and how they match the demands made on those abilities. Whether the child's problems indicate a disorder at all depends on the context, the demands on the child, the child's strengths as well as vulnerabilities and the support given.

The available data suggest that it is critical for the field to move beyond one-dimensional conceptualisations of the cause of AD/HD. Numerous researchers propose that both individual differences in the organic and psychological make-up of the child and individual differences in the family and social environment contribute to whether or not a child is identified as AD/HD. This multi-dimensional, dialectical model indicates a complex interaction between the child's environment and his or her physical and psychological status.

Comorbidities and Associated Problems

Being diagnosed as having AD/HD raises the odds of having several other problems as well – a phenomenon known as comorbidity. In particular, children with AD/HD may be more likely than others to have additional medical, developmental, behavioural, social, emotional and academic difficulties.

AD/HD children are more likely than others to have a specific learning difficulty, to be clumsy and to experience speech and language difficulties (Barkley 1995a, 1998; Du Paul and Stoner 1994; Tannock 1998). Between 20 per cent and 40 per cent of AD/HD children have at least one type of learning difficulty in reading, spelling or maths. Richards (1995) quotes American estimates that 33 per cent of AD/HD children can also be described as having reading problems.

Some studies have found that children with AD/HD are likely to be behind the general mental or intellectual development of non-AD/HD children to a not very large but still significant degree (Hinshaw 1992; Palkes and Stewart 1972; Sonuga-Barke et al. 1994). However, differences may be a reflection more of the problems AD/HD imposes on the test-taking abilities than of inherent intelligence. Children with AD/HD are likely to represent the whole spectrum of the normal range of intellectual development (Barkley 1995a).

Children with AD/HD are often described as immature and incompetent socially. They struggle to join an ongoing activity or conversation. They do not know how to take turns. Sociometric and play studies suggest that AD/HD children are not as often chosen by peers as best friends or partners in activities

(Pelham and Milich 1984). They may suffer from low self-esteem due to the recurrent negative feedback they receive (Barkley 1998).

Children with AD/HD seem to have more problems with their general health, and experience enuresis and poor sleeping patterns. Some studies have found that children with AD/HD are more accident prone (Barkley 1998).

AD/HD is often associated with other emotional and behavioural disorders. Up to 45 per cent of AD/HD children have at least one other psychiatric disorder besides AD/HD (Barkley 1995a). They are at risk of developing Oppositional Defiant and Conduct Disorders, making it difficult for their needs to be met in mainstream education. It is important for educators to realise that this course of events is avoidable if AD/HD is treated before the child develops serious social, emotional, behavioural and academic problems.

Why is AD/HD Difficult to Diagnose?

It is important for professionals to recognise that symptoms of inattentiveness and impulsiveness occur across a range of childhood problems. As Goldstein (1997) points out, inattention constitutes the most common symptom in all the DSM-IV disorders. A major issue thus for the clinician is one of differential diagnosis. This concerns the primacy of one disorder or syndrome over the other in cases in which both coexist. For instance, is a problem that is not AD/HD causing a child to present similar behaviour to an AD/HD child? Do one or more problems exist separately from one another but interact adversely upon one another (e.g. AD/HD and dyslexia/specific learning difficulties)? Is AD/HD giving rise to a secondary problem which is then having an adverse effect upon the AD/HD difficulties (e.g. anxiety disorder)? It is sometimes difficult to resolve whether a problem such as anxiety is the cause or the effect of AD/HD difficulties.

AD/HD is a medical diagnosis. However there is no evident medical test to account for it at the present moment. To make a diagnosis, one has to infer a medical condition from behavioural symptoms. The problem is that behavioural manifestations tap many different levels and are subject to many influences which include environmental and cognitive processes as well as purely biological ones. We must be alert to the danger of mistaking a symptom at the behavioural level for the inferred underlying trait or ability at the biological or cognitive level. One symptom is only a pointer. Multiple sampling and careful elimination of other reasons that could explain symptoms, increases the likelihood of an accurate diagnosis.

In most cases AD/HD probably represents the relatively extreme end of a normal dimension of a trait. It arises along a continuum such as height or weight rather than as a categorical condition such as pregnancy. Establishing the boundary of the 'clinically significant zone' for AD/HD is a thorny issue. As Barkley (1997) points out, it is as if one is trying to say exactly when day ends and night begins. Setting the line of demarcation along the dimension is inevitably going to be a bit arbitrary and more often the result of a consensus of opinion than some true cut-off score. That is not to say that establishing such a cut-off or boundary is unhelpful – far from it. Many decisions that are made about clinical cases are *categorical* in nature (to medicate or not to medicate). It is just that demarcation will more likely be decided by social and political considerations than by purely scientific ones.

Finally, the degree to which AD/HD is a handicap, and its development and course, depend not only on the severity of the symptoms but also on one's environment. In this context a child may be disabled but not necessarily handicapped if the environment is adaptable to the child's needs.

All of these issues, of course, are not exclusive to AD/HD alone but are also relevant to the definition and classification of all developmental and mental conditions that represent simply extreme points along the continuum of normality – for example moderate and severe learning difficulties, specific learning difficulties, depression, anxiety disorder, Tourette's syndrome, and pervasive developmental disorders such as autism and Asperger's syndrome.

The above considerations call for a careful and comprehensive assessment, including multi-modal and multi-method analysis which involves exclusionary as well as inclusionary criteria for diagnosis. This should include sampling data from different sources alongside a detailed developmental and family history documenting the onset, duration and pervasiveness of symptoms across contexts and settings.

Overview of AD/HD

Primary Symptoms

- ° Inattention
- ° Impulsivity
- ° Hyperactivity

Secondary Symptoms

- ° Behavioural difficulties
- ° Poor school achievement and or learning difficulties
- ° Poor peer relationships
- ° Low self-esteem

Cognitive Deficits

Inability to sustain attention and to inhibit impulsive responding on tasks or in social situations that require focused, reflective, self-directed effort.

Prevalence

There are huge discrepancies in reported incidence rates with approximately 0.03 per cent of schoolchildren treated with psychostimulants in the UK compared with 1 per cent in Australia and 3 per cent in the USA. However, some confusion arises from the fact that there are differential diagnostic criteria between the USA and UK counterparts for defining the type of disorder (see Appendix A).

Developmental Shifts in Symptoms

- ° ***Infancy:*** These children may have a history of prenatal and perinatal difficulties. Sleep disorder is common and can often date back to the early months of life. Early history often reveals a restless, irritable, crying baby who is difficult to settle and difficult to feed.

- ° ***Preschool years:*** Diagnosis in this age group is difficult, due to the wide range of normal behaviours manifest during this period. As toddlers and preschoolers, however, these children are even more active and exploratory than is typical for this developmental stage. They are likely to be more difficult to control and more likely to engage in difficult behaviours as a result of their impulsivity.

- ° ***Early school years:*** Difficulties in attention and concentration become more apparent as these children enter school. They appear to lack the capacity to modulate their attention and activity level to match the demands of the environment. Specific learning difficulties may emerge together with peer difficulties which contribute to low self-esteem.

- ° ***Adolescence:*** Hyperactivity may decline during teenage years although difficulties with attention, impulsivity and excitability are likely to persist. These adolescents are at risk of developing Oppositional and Conduct Disorders, making it difficult for their needs to be met in mainstream education. Without intervention secondary problems mentioned above may become more pronounced.

o *Adulthood*: Research indicates that difficulties continue into adulthood for 60 per cent and may be associated with other emotional and behavioural concerns.

Theories of Causation

o *Biological*: Neurological and/or biochemical processes may be involved.

o *Bioenvironmental*: An interaction of the individual's biology with some type of environmental agent may be involved.

o *Environmental*: Dysfunctional social environments, families and school may contribute to the child's inattention and overactivity.

CHAPTER 3

Diagnosis and Assessment Considerations

The previous chapter has already touched on some of the difficulties inherent in making a diagnosis of AD/HD. What then are the critera necessary for a diagnosis of AD/HD? These are detailed in Appendix A and are outlined below.

In order to be considered to be present, the symptoms of AD/HD must:

° have an **onset** prior to 7 years of age,

° have a **duration** of *at least 6 months*, and

° be **evident** to a degree that is *developmentally deviant.*

There must also be clear evidence that these symptoms cause functional impairment across *two or more settings* in which the individual functions. Above and beyond these inclusionary criteria, the guidelines also require *ruling out* certain conditions that might better account for the presence of such symptomatology. In particular they cannot be the exclusive result of disorders such as autism, schizophrenia or psychosis and must not be better accounted for by a diagnosis of a mood, anxiety, or personality disorder.

Based on these criteria children can be diagnosed as:

- **AD/HD predominantly inattentive type**, *if the inattention but not the hyperactive impulsive criteria are met*

- **AD/HD predominantly hyperactive-impulsive type**, *if the hyperactive, impulsive – but not the inattentive – criteria are met*

- **AD/HD combined type**, *if both sets of criteria are met*

   N.b. AD/HD in Partial Remission is specified for individuals (especially adolescents and adults) who have symptoms that no longer meet the full criteria.

Assessment for AD/HD requires the employment of multiple methods of data collection across informants and settings. In particular, emphasis is placed upon obtaining reliable information about the child's behaviour from parents and teachers as well as from first-hand observations. Diagnosing AD/HD can be a tricky business. To make a careful diagnosis one must eliminate other explanations for the symptoms. The goal is not simply to arrive at a diagnosis of AD/HD, but to determine an intervention plan that is likely to succeed, based on the information gathered.

Major components of the evaluation should include:

- Interview with parents

- Psychological and school evaluation

- Clinical and medical examination.

Information from the following areas should be gathered in order to assess for AD/HD:

- Developmental and Family History

- Behaviour Across Settings

- Review of School/Preschool Records

- Individual Psychological Assessment and Cognitive Profile
- Clinical and Medical Examination.

Developmental and Family History

Parent interviews form the basis of information-gathering here. Parents have a unique perspective on their child's development and current adjustments, as they have witnessed the child in a variety of situations over a number of years. Consequently, information should be sought providing a detailed family history of which the focus is usually description of family structure and functioning and documentation of important events from the child's medical, developmental, social and academic history. Problem behaviours should be inappropriate when compared to those of other children of the same mental age and examined in the context of maturational changes. Getting parents to tell and reflect on life history can also be used as a powerful therapeutic tool of the assessment process: it can help them to gain insight into the child's difficulties and their contribution in management and effecting change.

Behaviour Across Settings

There must be clear evidence that symptoms cause functional impairment across two or more settings – typically home and school. Information can be gathered through reports or interviews as well as direct observation of the child across settings.

Rating scales can be used to provide valid, reliable data from these different settings. Comparisons can be made between parent and teacher ratings on a number of dimensions. A whole number of different rating scales are available. Of these, the Achenbach rating scales are generally recognised to be one of the most valid and reliable psychometric checklists available

(Achenbach 1991). They take account of age and sex and separate forms exist for the child, parent and teacher. They provide a profile of eight syndrome scales – including *Attention Problems* – which can be computer scored and analysed with percentiles and clinical significance levels. Responses between individuals can easily be compared. Excellent convergence has been found between dimensions on this scale and the diagnosis of ADHD in the research literature (Biederman *et al.* 1993).

Other rating scales include: Conners' Rating Scales – Revised (Conners 1997); Attention Comprehensive Teachers' Rating Scale: ACTeRS (Ullman, Sleator and Sprague 1991); Barkley Home and School Situations Questionnaires – Revised (Barkley 1991a); Brown ADD Scales (Brown 1997).

Systematic classroom observation schedules can also be used to provide objective information regarding the frequencies of various AD/HD-related behaviours across tasks and situations. Behaviours here should be compared to a control subject from the child's peer group. Again various schedules are available and can be tailored to individual needs and circumstances (see Croll 1986; Goldstein 1995).

It is important to remember that all questionnaires and rating scales are subjective and care is needed in their interpretation. Furthermore, while questionnaires and rating scales differentiate well between AD/HD children and controls, they are less good at differentiating between AD/HD and other areas of special need, for example between AD/HD and speech and language difficulties. Good clinical skills of interviewing and judgement which elicit reliable data from respondents who witness the child's behaviour across settings and across time spans are essential components for any diagnosis.

Review of School Records

School records and interventions should be reviewed to pinpoint the onset and course of AD/HD-related difficulties and response to interventions. Assessment for AD/HD should include information about the student's current and past classroom performance, academic strengths and weaknesses, and other social, emotional or behavioural characteristics. The student's adjustment should relate to aspects of the curriculum in which the student is working: teacher expectations for the class and for the individual student, methods of instruction employed, incentives for work completion and comparative performance of other students in the class. Assessment here follows a staged process similar to the Code of Practice on the assessment of special educational needs (Department for Education 1994 – see sec.5).

Individual Psychological Assessment and Cognitive Profile

A psychological evaluation essentially follows a problem-solving framework. A full cognitive assessment is not necessarily required if observational data alongside evidence from the school did not implicate AD/HD type symptoms. Where AD/HD type symptoms are implicated, assessment of cognitive profile is valuable in determining the child's capacities in various domains of cognitive functioning. A psychologist will need to administer and interpret psychological and educational tests of cognition, perception, and language development as well as tests of achievement and social/emotional adjustment. Particular consideration will need to be given to assessing attention span, visual-motor skills, memory, impulsivity, planning and organisational skills. Results of such tests can provide important clues as to whether a child's difficulties are related to AD/HD and/or other problems with learning, behaviour or emotional adjustment.

Tests of cognitive ability may be administered to assess whether or not the child is under-achieving, to observe learning style and to look for any other areas of dysfunction. The diagnosis of AD/HD requires that the child's behaviour be inconsistent with their cognitive age or level (Barkley 1998; Braswell and Bloomquist 1991). For instance, if the child's attentional capacities appear more like those of someone much younger, then this observation might lead to an appropriate diagnosis of AD/HD if the child's cognitive capacities are at age level or advanced. If, however, the child's performance suggests that he or she is exhibiting delays across all aspects of intellectual functioning, then assigning a diagnosis of AD/HD may be inappropriate if the child's attentional capacities are actually in line with their other cognitive capabilities.

Clinical profile and observations of learning style and behaviour are as relevant as any overall score of intellectual functioning. For instance, children with AD/HD typically (but not always) tend to have low scores on the Freedom from Distractibility and Processing Speed factors from the Wechsler Intelligence Scale for Children (Kaufman 1994; Schwean and Saklofske 1998; Wechsler 1992). It is interesting to note that in the research literature AD/HD children have been found to perform no differently from controls on tasks requiring automatic or relatively effortless processing; but on tasks requiring increasing levels of organisation in attention and/or memory, AD/HD children perform worse than both normals and reading-disabled, nonhyperactive controls (August 1987; Borcherding et al. 1988; Tant and Douglas 1982).

The Continuous Performance Test (CPT) initially devised by Rosvold et. al. (1956) is a test of vigilance and impulsivity and has computerised versions which are used by many clinicians as a diagnostic marker for AD/HD. Some debate exists, however, as to whether the instrument reliably discriminates between AD/HD and normal controls as it is subject to other variables such as task parameters, selection criteria, situational and external factors which may have an impact on performance (Corkum and Siegel 1993; Corkum and Siegel 1995; Koelega 1995).

The American Academy of Child and Adolescent Psychiatry (1997) reached the following conclusions:

- ° Behavioural observations of children performing the CPT discriminate AD/HD children from controls as well as, or better than, the CPT scores.

- ° A correspondence between impulsive errors on the CPT and behavioural impulsivity has not been established.

- ° When used to assess the efficacy of medication, it is not yet proven that the results on the CPT generalise to the natural environment.

- ° CPTs are not consistently sensitive to stimulant effects.

- ° CPTs are sensitive to differences in administration, and protocols have not been developed for their use.

To date, no individually administered test or group of tests has demonstrated an acceptable degree of ecological validity in the diagnostic process (Barkley 1991b, 1995b, 1997, 1998; Du Paul and Stoner 1994; Tannock 1998; Taylor 1994a, 1994b). There is no particular intelligence test profile to discriminate AD/HD reliably from normal children or other students with learning difficulties (Barkley, DuPaul and McMurray 1990; Barkley 1997). For instance, scores on the Freedom from Dis-tractibility factor of the WISC-III are not reliable diagnostic indicators of AD/HD (Cohen, Becker and Campbell 1990). Poor performance on this factor may be due to a variety of possible causes, including performance anxiety. Furthermore, children with AD/HD often display appropriate levels of attention and behavioural control under task conditions that are highly structured and involve one-to-one interaction with an unfamiliar adult. Nevertheless, individually administered tests are helpful in providing a clinical and cognitive profile which informs both the assessment and intervention process (Barkley

1998; Taylor 1994b). The goal of the evaluation is not simply to arrive at a diagnosis of AD/HD, but to determine an intervention plan that is likely to succeed, based upon the information gathered.

Clinical and Medical Examination

It is essential that children being considered for a diagnosis of AD/HD have a complete paediatric physical examination (Barkley 1981, 1998). Time will also need to be devoted to a thorough review of family background history, pre- and perinatal events, developmental and medical history as well as to the child's current health, nutritional status and sensory-motor development.

A major focus of the medical interview is on the differential diagnosis of AD/HD from other medical and psychological conditions, particularly those that may be treatable. In some cases the AD/HD may have arisen as a result of an adverse biological event – such as hypoxia (lack of oxygen), significant head trauma, central nervous system infection or cerebral-vascular disease. It is also necessary to determine whether the child's difficulties are related to the emergence of epilepsy.

Another purpose of the medical examination is to evaluate any co-existing conditions that may require medical management. As already outlined, AD/HD is often associated with higher risks for a whole number of other conditions. Children with epilepsy or significant allergies such as asthma will require careful evaluation because of the behavioural side effects of medications used to treat them.

It is also necessary to determine whether physical conditions exist that are contraindications for treatment with medications (e.g. high blood pressure, Tourette's syndrome). While routine physical examinations of AD/HD children are frequently normal, one certainly needs to rule out physical factors such as visual or hearing deficits that may give rise to symptoms of

AD/HD. Accurate baseline data on physical growth, heart rate and blood pressure will be needed against which to compare subsequently if medication is to be contemplated.

All of this data will need to be considered within the context of an assessment of family functioning and parenting strategies alongside other relevant environmental and social factors.

Integrating Assessment Data

Although each assessment technique has limitations, the advantages of using a multi-method approach is that each technique's strengths and weaknesses will be balanced out as part of a larger evaluation package (Du Paul and Stoner 1994). The goal is to derive consistent information regarding the frequency and severity of related behaviours across contexts and their persistence across the child's development, which are critical in identifying what is essentially a syndrome in childhood as AD/HD.

The current state of knowledge strongly suggests that professionals must rely on several methods of assessment, utilise several sources of information from different settings, and interpret the data obtained within both a biopsychosocial and a developmental perspective.

Integrating the information collected should lead to an understanding of the child's physical, cognitive, academic, be-havioural and emotional strengths and weaknesses which inform interventions and treatment planning. Behaviour modification, cognitive therapy, counselling, social and organisational skills training are examples of options which can be used. For many, medical treatment is critical to the child's ability to function.

No single treatment is likely to deal effectively with the cluster of behaviours and problems that these children experience. It is really a matter of defining the problem, the behaviour and the situations in which the problems occur, and then looking at a repertoire of interventions.

CHAPTER 4

Interventions at School

Treatment approaches should be multimodal and include the following elements according to the needs of the individual child:

- ° knowledge and understanding of AD/HD
- ° family support and intervention
- ° school intervention and management programmes
- ° behaviour management programmes
- ° individual cognitive approaches
- ° medication.

These points are incorporated in the following guidelines in this and the following chapters, relating to school, home and medical interventions.

School Based Strategies and Interventions for Children Diagnosed as Having AD/HD

Many impulsive and hyperactive children can be supported in a mainstream class by the employment of the following ideas and strategies. It would also be true to say that what will help a child with AD/HD could help many children. It will be important to prevent the child feeling or being rejected by his or her peers as this may exacerbate the situation. Consideration of the learning environment with this in mind can reduce the high profile nature of the behaviour. The strategies are aimed at inclusion wherever possible and we would encourage teachers to be creative in designing and implementing their own bank of ideas and resources – all aimed at supporting the child in accessing the curriculum. It would help if the diagnosing or labelling of the child did not equate with the perception of the child being deficient in some way. Diagnosis could lead to opportunities.

All teaching staff may need information and education about AD/HD and clarity about the reality and myths surrounding it. The class teacher may need positive support and understanding based on a shared experience and input.

Prescribed medication may support the initiatives, but the initiatives need to be in the child and teacher's repertoire in order to be used and produce positive outcomes.

The multi-professional dialogue and exchange of information will help to establish interventions that are effective. This will engage children with themselves, the curriculum, their peers, and home and family.

[N.b. Discretion and professional judgement will be needed to discriminate between strategies appropriate for primary or secondary pupils.]

Classroom Management

Classroom Organisation

Children with AD/HD require high levels of structure. The aim will be to plan and prepare a supportive learning environment that will enable an AD/HD child to feel comfortable, valued and understood. Academic success and progress is as important to an AD/HD child as any other. This is the basis for good practice for all children.

1. A structured daily routine where school can be a predictable place is reassuring. Any changes or alterations to the timetable need to be anticipated as far as possible in order to prepare the child.

2. Encourage all the children to keep their homework diary up to date (where appropriate) and ask to see their entries.

3. Set up a quiet area for the child with AD/HD (and others) to use at certain times.

Physical Arrangements

1. Attention to the seating and layout of furniture in the classroom will ensure that distractions are at a minimum. The child with AD/HD will need to sit in clear view of the teacher, the board, and near positive role models, and away from 'routes' around the room.

2. Keep desk clear of unwanted equipment. Encourage all children to keep working areas tidy.

3. Sit the child away from window catches, blinds, plugs and sockets etc.

Lesson Presentation

1. The child can be supported in aiming to increase his or her concentration and attention span through appropriate tasks and activities.

2. Focus on a positive outcome in order to complete tasks, rather than what still hasn't been done.

3. Foster and stimulate motivation, and think what helps the child with AD/HD to be engaged in the task.

4. Try out and practise finely tuned questions that will help to re-engage the child in the task. They will also act as a signal if the child and teacher have agreed what such questions mean.

5. Children with AD/HD have difficulty in screening out background noise. Keep noise level down to an acceptable level. Working in silence for short periods for specific tasks may be beneficial. Headphones will block auditory distractions.

6. Reward task completion. Do not allow unfinished assignments to mount up and overwhelm the child.

7. Teach children to take notes in class.

Managing Behaviours

1. Give simple clear targets which are understood by the child.

2. Class rules are important, to give information about teacher expectations. Rules should be positive, clearly displayed and referred to, and there should be no more than five.

3. There should be emphasis on frequent reinforcement of positive behaviour. Feedback needs to be immediate and related to specific behaviours. A rewards menu will give the child a degree of choice each time.

4. A clear hierarchy of sanctions will enable the child to receive information about their behaviour and the 'next step'. Include planned ignoring and time out (specified length) in the hierarchy.

5. Be aware, and make a record whenever possible of antecedents. This may give information leading to a change or modification of 'trigger'.

6. Support and encourage positive attention.

7. Communicate with the child in an assertive manner without using ridicule, lecture or criticism.

8. Try not to force the child into a corner; leave a way out. Try to end interaction on a positive note.

9. Encourage the child to 'put things right'.

10. Sort out non-compliance from incompetence, i.e. 'I can't' from 'I won't'. The latter needs a reprimand or sanction. The former needs to be taught.

11. Maintain a sense of priorities. Focus on no more than three behaviours at once.

12. Ignore inappropriate behaviour in order to inhibit these behaviours from being used for negative attention.

Social Skills

Children with AD/HD will benefit from friendships as much as any other child. Sometimes friendship skills are inadequate or inappropriate. These skills need to be taught within the context of the whole class.

1. Build and plan peer support by using ideas such as 'Circle of Friends' or a buddy support system. Careful monitoring will prevent peers becoming 'overpowered' by a child with AD/HD.

2. Teaching conflict resolution strategies or assertiveness for all children in order to build and raise the skill level of everyone.

3. Group work may be difficult and groups will need some input and support to minimise difficulties. Manage flexible groupings to ensure that children with AD/HD work with a variety of other children.

4. Initiatives such as peer tutoring, reading/writing, or spelling partners will need to be monitored and rotated.

5. Tutorial groups, Circle-time and similar projects enable self-esteem and social skills aspects to be covered.

6. Encourage seeing situations from another's viewpoint.

7. Model appropriate social skills. Model positive comments about work, attributes and interactions.

8. Foster the ethos that everyone is a worthwhile member of the group. Promote harmony in class.

Teaching Style

1. The steps to learning need to be small. Targets need to be realistic and achievable.

2. Planning for academic success is important.

3. In giving instructions to the class it may help to write a daily menu. Break down complex instructions into small chunks. Ask the child to tell you what they have to do. For young children instructions may need to be one at a time.

4. Give frequent feedback to the child on tasks and teach the child to assess and evaluate their work.

5. Follow-on tasks could motivate a child to complete non-favoured tasks. Variety is important.

6. With young children, sessions sitting on the carpet need to be kept short. With older children using only a didactic style of teaching may not be helpful.

7. Allow oral responses.

8. Reduce written requirements.

9. Teach discussion skills for all children. This will provide some positive modelling for the child with AD/HD. Allow the child to contribute to discussion more often.

10. Stay calm. Be aware of body language and tone of voice. This needs to reassure and inform not threaten and confuse.

11. When talking to the whole class, stand near the child and use their book, worksheet, etc. as an example.

12. Set tasks initially that can be completed quickly.

Individual Needs

Children with AD/HD frequently have low self-esteem with consequent avoidance of classwork because of fear of failure. They may have difficulties in performance not ability. If tasks are not completed satisfactorily, the work set may need to be less in amount, not easier. A focus on the positive attributes and achievements will be helpful.

1. Involve the child in possible solutions to problems. Try out ideas, evaluate them and be prepared to change them and try out something else if it doesn't work.

2. Look at systems that teach the child to self-record behaviour. Targets should be realistic and achievable and changed when achieved.

3. Presentation of work may not be acceptable. Some input in organisation and layout will help, as will use of the computer for final pieces.

4. Teach coping strategies for difficult times such as changing for PE, going to lunch, change of lessons.

5. Anxiety about poor performance or arising difficulties may be a factor. Teach relaxation techniques, and tips to deal with stress.

6. A child with AD/HD may have difficulty in selecting information. Study skills will need to be taught and reminders and prompts given on how to begin.

7. Writing could be a problem. Try asking for one sentence to begin with and then a list. Sequence of events or procedures may be hard to remember.

8. In spelling, ten words may be too many to learn. Select a small number then increase gradually.

9. In maths, for example, rather than asking for 20 problems to be solved, try asking for the first 3, followed by numbers 11 and 12 and the last 2.

10. Project or topic work is usually fairly open ended. A child with AD/HD may need structure and closer supervision. Small manageable pieces of work may be more realistic.

11. Teach the child to anticipate pitfalls or identify the parts they can manage and the parts with which they may need help.

12. Children with AD/HD have a tendency to forget and they may need more reminders than others.

13. Encourage eye contact, without insisting.

14. Use a range of ways of recording such as:

   ° word processor

   ° dictaphone or tape recorder

   ° diagrams

   ° graphs

   ° pictorial representation

   ° adult scribe

   ° writing partner.

15. Frustration may be alleviated by frequent reassurance or short breaks during the day, such as taking a message or finding a resource.

16. Encourage the child to look for mental pictures of concepts or information. Visualisation helps.

17. Use a timer to help with deadlines.

18. Clumsiness and awkward fine motor skills will need to be sensitively handled. Be realistic about what is to be achieved.

19. Try encouraging the child to use a piece of card with a window cut into it to focus on one small part of the text at a time.

20. Photocopy text, when appropriate, and teach the child to use a highlighter pen to extract main points.

21. Teach children to organise themselves. Checklists for resources may be helpful and the child can tick them off as they go. If these are laminated they can be re-used.

22. Children with AD/HD may not need too much repetition but more variety.

Home and School

1. Parents need to know about school routines, expectations and should even be given a copy of the timetable. This will enable them to assist the child in organisation.

2. Using a home–school message book will help communication (this is not used for recording difficult incidents).

3. Encourage parents to have a routine that helps the child check and pack bag each night ready for the morning.

4. Communication with parents needs to be effective. Effective and positive strategies can be shared.

5. The school's behaviour management system could have a joint focus that gives some continuity and consistency.

6. For young children the handover each morning and evening needs to be tight and clear. Daily inquisitions between teacher and parent are not helpful. This exchange could be weekly or even fortnightly. It is important to focus on the positives and achievements.

7. School outings or educational visits may require extra supervision.

8. Allow parents to initial homework when specified time has been spent on the assignment.

9. Emphasise parent–teacher partnership. Support works best when it is mutual.

10. Involve the parents in target-setting with their child.

11. Ensure liaison exists between all who work with the child, ensuring targets are appropriate and realistic.

12. Review targets regularly.

13. Celebrate success.

Summary

Children with AD/HD can be exhausting class members. Try to keep a disability perspective. The effective learning environment for the child with AD/HD will be one that supports individual difference within a flexible, structured approach and not one that focuses on the difference whereby they become alienated. It will help to be proactive in dealing with a child with AD/HD and not reactive. The whole school can be educated into understanding and responding to the child as achievements and successes are celebrated and valued. Children with AD/HD respond well to a caring attitude of their educators and will thrive as a result.

CHAPTER 5

Interventions at Home

Just as they need educational success, children with AD/HD must have sufficient personal success in their life if they are to develop their ability and be able to succeed in their world. All children with AD/HD are different and for parents struggling with the day-to-day difficulties and dramas of AD/HD, emotions can run high. Even the world's best parents can feel inadequate, guilty, disappointed or downright angry. It is thus essential for parents to look at their own needs and concerns as well as those of their child and to seek advice in coping with their feelings and those of other family members. A good outcome for children with AD/HD can be expected if parents (or other carers) are understanding, supportive and use confident and consistent positive parenting.

The following represent guidelines for parents in the home management of children with AD/HD (more detailed descriptions can be found in the references at the end of this book). Many of the same guidelines for teachers from the previous section can also be applied to the home situation. These are not meant to be exhaustive or applicable in every incidence to all children with AD/HD. Not one management strategy in and of itself is likely to deal effectively with what is essentially a cluster of behaviours and problems which these children exhibit.

Develop Knowledge and Understanding

AD/HD is part of the child's make-up. It is not a disease but a pattern of problem behaviour, much of which is largely outside their control. It does not have a single cause or a single cure and the first step is to understand and accept the problem because no amount of pushing or punishing will make the child behave perfectly. Developing parental understanding of the problems which children with AD/HD exhibit is an important step in their home management.

Parents need to maintain a disability perspective where they are not unduly criticising or punishing the child for things they cannot do. They need to develop an understanding the distinction between of what their children 'can't do' and what they 'won't do'. For the most part these children are not intentionally misbehaving. If they are, then the behaviour needs to be punished and not the child. Parents need to help the child to see that it is what he or she does, not who he or she is, that is unacceptable. In dealing with difficult behaviour, a good maxim is to remember to criticise the behaviour and value the individual.

Think and Act Positively About your Child

Children with AD/HD need to see consequences for their behaviour which are predictable, salient and clear, and to gain feedback far more frequently and quickly than other children do, if they are to maintain control over their behaviour. Both secondary rewards (praise) and primary rewards (toys, treats or privileges) must be provided at a higher rate when children with AD/HD are co-operative or succeed. Parents need to remember that it is likely that the child with AD/HD receives fewer positive responses than siblings and they may need to make an effort to keep the scales balanced.

If the child is not receiving positive attention he or she will work to receive negative attention.   If the consequences of behaviour are rewarding (that is favourable) to a child, that behaviour is likely to increase. Where an undesirable behaviour is not reinforced or underplayed it will probably not happen again. The aim is to be a positive parent, to monitor, comment on and reward the good and desirable behaviour.

How do you do this?

(1)   Make praise contingent on behaviour.

(2)   Praise immediately.

(3)   Give labelled and specific praise.

(4)   Give positive praise without qualifiers or sarcasm.

(5)   Praise with smiles, eye contact and enthusiasm as well as with words.

(6)   Give pats, hugs and kisses along with verbal praise.

(7)   Catch the child whenever he or she is being good; don't save praise for perfect behaviour only.

(8)   Use praise consistently whenever you see the positive behaviour you want to encourage.

(9)   Praise in front of other children.

Regardless of the difficulties, it is important for parents to maintain a positive relationship with their child. They should try to find an enjoyable activity and engage in this activity with their child as often as possible, at least a couple of times each week. Letting the child choose the 'special time' activity and take the lead can increase self-confidence.

Develop a Positive Self-Esteem for your Child

Children with AD/HD may end up feeling fairly negative about their ability to be able to succeed in their world and be unable to accept and recognise things they do well. That is not surprising; because of their learning history they simply do not have the same experiences as other children. These children cannot be over-praised for effort and good behaviour as their self-esteem is often poor. They may need help to take a critical look at themselves by focusing on their successes and so modify their feelings and self-esteem. They need to be taught to be positive by their parents, who need to say positive things to their children every day – for the rest of their lives if necessary.

Children with AD/HD are often creative and have special talents. Their strengths must be recognised and used, even if their talents do not always fit parental hopes and expectations. Discovering, highlighting and nurturing areas of competence can be a very positive way of improving the child's self-esteem.

Implement Routine, Structure and Predictability

Children with AD/HD benefit from predictability and structure at home. Distinct schedules for getting up in the morning, doing homework in the evening, and fulfilling daily obligations have a beneficial impact. A preset routine for homework helps establish good study habits. Ideally, there should be no television or other distraction permitted during these homework hours. Gradually, children should be expected to assume their responsibilities in a predictable manner.

Children with AD/HD also benefit from parents setting clear and consistent boundaries for unacceptable behaviour. A child with AD/HD must be sure of where he or she stands; they cannot cope when the ground rules keep changing. Parents should make sure children know the rules and how they are to follow them; they need to be told of any changes to routine and any change should be planned in advance.

Both parents or partners must have similar policies and reactions to the child's various actions. This may require considerable discussion and planning. With older children it can be helpful to include them in decisions about family rules, rewards and sanctions. By being included, children begin to learn longer-term problem-solving strategies.

Communicate Clearly

Children who are inattentive, impulsive and apparently deaf to discipline need the clearest communication and instruction. Instruction should be clear, concise and consistently reinforced. Expecting the child to exert self-discipline is unrealistic and will often end in confrontation, which is not helpful. Positive instruction, such as 'Put your feet on the floor', rather than 'Don't put your feet on the table', have more effect.

Make sure children know the rules and what they are to follow.

Parents often find it hard to be really firm with their children. If the child has got into the habit of paying no attention to their instructions, they may have to practise some or all the following in order to make sure he or she listens to what they are asked to do:

(1) Hold him or her still by the shoulders while you give the instruction.

(2) Look into his or her eyes.

(3) Talk in a clear and firm.

(4) Insist on being attended to and obeyed for a reasonable instruction.

(5) Remember that mumbling, nagging, debating, pleading, shouting and talking over the television will get you nowhere.

(6) It will be helpful to have the child repeat your request.

Take Control

As adults, parents need to remember that they have the right to control the situation. They should avoid letting the child 'get to them' and making them annoyed. They should not use threats that cannot he carried out. Criticism needs to be tempered with praise each day. The goal should be to increase the frequency of praise so that 'good' behaviour is encouraged.

Parents should avoid making personal remarks which may hurt children. They will lose their child's respect and damage their relationship with them. They should try not to be sarcastic or aggressive. All children imitate their parents' behaviour, and children with AD/HD are no exception.

Confrontation is best avoided as many children with AD/HD will seek attention even if it is negative. Conflict should be resolved quickly and wherever possible privately. An opportunity to succeed should quickly follow. Parents should try to make sure that interactions end successfully. Children should not be left with no way out. If the child feels cornered there is a danger of confrontation. A 'better for both' solution is preferable. Sometimes (especially with older children) it is better to compromise and modify a behaviour pattern rather than expecting to banish it completely.

Have Realistic Expectations

Parents should not escalate problems by rising to unimportant irritations but focus on the few big behaviours that matter most. It is important to have realistic expectations and make allowances. Parents should not attempt to deal with all the child's undesirable behaviours at the same time. They should select no more than one or two behaviours that at any one time are most in need of careful management and work on these exclusively or primarily. The selection of these behaviours depends largely on the family priorities and the extent to which the behaviours are likely to have damaging long-term consequences on the child (e.g. hitting other children).

Set Up Sanctions ('Safety Valves')

There comes a point in managing a child with AD/HD where parents see things are rapidly escalating out of control. Once a behaviour gets past this point there ceases to be any place for reason or rational thinking. Now is the time to back off and put in place sanctions which can reduce the emotional temperature and act as safety valves for child and parent.

(1) Planned Ignoring

(i)   Parents should take absolutely no notice of behaviours such as rude remarks and protests.

(ii) Parents should ignore tantrums, shouts and screams by wherever possible leaving the child without an audience.

(iii) Parents should get on with their own affairs, e.g. get out the Hoover so the child's tantrums cannot be heard.

(iv) If it is really important that the child obeys parents, they should show the child that they mean what they say: by making eye contact and repeating instructions with a raised (not screaming) and firm voice (it is all right to look really angry!).

(2) Time-Out

Time-out is a technique where by a deteriorating situation can be salvaged by briefly removing the child from all attention and audience. For example, a period of isolation in the bedroom might be effective. This should only be for a short time, one possible rule of thumb being that the child should remain in time-out for one minute for every year of his or her life, up to a maximum of ten minutes. Only when quiet, even though not openly repentant, should the child be allowed to return to the real world. Time-out should be reserved for behaviour which cannot realistically be ignored (e.g. aggression). It is a complicated technique and generally works better with younger children. It will not be effective if the child enjoys the time, so toys and activities should not be available in the time-out setting. Parents should take the earliest opportunity to praise the child once the time-out period is over.

Take Care of Yourself

Children with AD/HD can generate immense stress in their families, yet stress is the number one catalyst for setting off bad behaviour. It is important, whether it is easy or not, to keep calm. Parents need to remember their own needs and those of other children too. Time away (respite), adult company and outside interests can all help to reduce the stress level for parents and siblings.

Seek Advice

Anticipating every possible scenario in the home life of a child with AD/HD is not feasible. Parents may require counselling to help them with day-to-day management issues. Advice should be given by someone who has a good understanding of AD/HD, otherwise parents are likely to feel blamed, leading to needless guilt or accusation.

Psychological or therapeutic input should address the child's emotional problems within the family context. Behaviour management programmes can (and should) be carefully designed to suit the values and needs of the family. The resulting therapy plan should be the outcome of a collaborative partnership between parents and therapist.

CHAPTER 6

Medication

Perhaps the single issue which has created the most controversy about AD/HD is the use of medication in its treatment. This can raise strong emotions, particularly when schools are asked to become involved in the administration of medication.

Methylphenidate (Ritalin) has been the most commonly used and studied medication for AD/HD in childhood. Surveys suggest that 90 to 95 per cent of prescriptions for AD/HD are written for methylphenidate in the USA. Its effects are dramatic for approximately 75 per cent of children exhibiting symptoms of hyperactivity, inattention, and impulsive behaviour. Furthermore, aggressive, antisocial, and oppositional problems, as well as peer and parental relations, are improved.

Methylphenidate is generally *ineffective* for symptoms related to anxiety, conduct disorder, or mood disorders; it has inconsistent effects on learning and does not on its own necessarily increase academic skills other than the improvement which is seen because of better attention and reduced distractibility. Medication does not teach new skills, but it may provide a window of opportunity for careful teaching to take place.

Long-term studies suggest that the benefits of medication usually disappear quickly after treatment is discontinued.

Some children do not respond and, in a few, behaviour can become worse or they become depressed and languid, in which case the medication will be discontinued or the dose reduced.

Methylphenidate acts as a stimulant to produce more of the likely deficiencies of neurotransmitter substances found in children with AD/HD. Messages can then travel more smoothly. It is likely that around puberty the inevitable hormone changes produce a natural 'catch up' in many of these children who have up to this time been deficient. It is noted that methylphenidate is not a tranquilliser or a sedative. It is in fact a stimulant medication assisting the brain to produce what is relatively lacking.

Side Effects

Side effects are few. In some children there is a suppression of appetite and the possibility of weight loss. For this reason the medication is taken with food. Other side effects can include some initial fatigue, occasional headache, occasional dizziness and, in exceptional cases, some blurring of vision. All these side effects usually do not last for more than a few days before they dissipate as the child adjusts to the medication.

Methylphenidate can cause insomnia, slow growth and a few children develop tics. This is unusual and is rarely seen in the doses recommended.

Addiction

In children the medication is not addictive. Some children may become a little weepy as the medication is wearing off. This is a temporary effect and is thought to be related to the fact that neurotransmitter substances also influence mood change and when depleted or present in insufficient amounts may be related to depression. If this effect is observed, and it is not common, it wears off within a few weeks.

Long-term studies have failed to demonstrate an increased likelihood of drug addiction, alcoholism, criminality, or growth suppression.

The Treatment Decision

The standard medical model for treatment decision making requires a comparison of the risks and benefits of any treatment with alternative choices. Several factors may contribute to a decision to use medication for AD/HD symptoms in children: severity of symptoms; presence of comorbid disorders; effectiveness of non-medication interventions; the child's compliance and tolerance for pharmacological intervention.

The need for treatment is also influenced by the presence of other disorders. For example, if a child with AD/HD has a severe episode of depression or shows symptoms of epilepsy, treatment of the depression or epilepsy should usually take precedence over treatment of AD/HD (Goldstein and Goldstein 1995).

Medication is only one aspect of management. Parents and teachers should be advised about management techniques first and the response evaluated before considering medication.

Follow-Up

After treatment has been initiated, careful follow-up is essential, initially by phone if necessary and then at an interval of 4–6 weeks followed by 3–6 monthly reviews. This is necessary in order to gauge the effect the medication is having on the child's attention, learning and behaviour as well as monitoring weight, pulse and blood pressure. Yearly full blood counts should be performed. Appropriate questionnaires should be completed by parents and schools. Global rating scales, direct patient observation, and qualitative reports can also be used to determine the effectiveness of treatment. Psychopharmacological treatment should continue to be accompanied by appropriate psychosocial interventions. For this reason, it is imperative that there is close co-operation between parents, teachers, medical personnel and psychologists. Medication should not be used as the initial or sole treatment strategy for the management of AD/HD.

CHAPTER 7

Educational Provision
AD/HD and the SEN Code of Practice

The Code of Practice on the Identification and Assessment of Special Educational Needs (Department for Education 1994) applies to cases, or suspected cases, of AD/HD in the same way as it applies to every other type of special educational need. The Code stipulates the adoption of the following five-stage model.

Stage 1: class or subject teachers identify or register a child's special educational needs and take initial action

Stage 2: the school's Special Educational Needs (SEN) co-ordinator takes lead responsibility for gathering information and for co-ordinating the child's special educational provision, working with the child's teachers

Stage 3: teachers and the SEN co-ordinator are supported by specialists from outside the school

Stage 4: the Local Education Authority (LEA) consider the need for a statutory assessment and, if appropriate, make a multi-disciplinary assessment

Stage 5: the LEA consider the need for a statement of special educational needs and, if appropriate, make a statement and arrange, monitor and review provision.

An educational psychologist will usually be involved at Stage 3. If AD/HD is suspected, but not medically diagnosed, specialist advice must also be sought from the appropriate health service personnel (consultant paediatrician/child and family psychiatrist) via the GP.

Whether or not a child with AD/HD will pass through all school-based stages of assessment and provision will depend upon the extent of the child's difficulties and how he or she responds to the measures taken to overcome or alleviate them.

Before the LEA could consider a statutory assessment, at Stage 4, there would need to be evidence that:

○ the pupil, after receiving counselling and assistance from personnel within school, still exhibits contextually inappropriate behaviour

○ the pupil, after systematic intervention conducted for a reasonable period (usually at least one term) based on the advice of an educational psychologist continues to exhibit inappropriate behaviour. This evidence would include the systematic measurement of the behaviour concerned and indicate that the intervention had failed to significantly modify the target behaviour.

In this context 'significantly modify the target behaviour' means that a change in behaviour has been demonstrated to such a degree that, with continuation of the intervention programme by the ordinary class teacher and input from services and provision normally available at the school, the pupil could continue within the ordinary classroom and have full access to the National Curriculum.

For a Statement to be issued at Stage 5 there would need to be evidence that the child's difficulties are significant, that they are likely to be long-term and that they impair the quality of his or her development, or that of other children.   There will be resulting under-achievement in normal social contexts with failure of social development and integration.

LEA provision for children with AD/HD who have Statements of Special Need will vary according to the extent and nature of the presenting difficulties and whether the child has other special needs which do not result from AD/HD.

LEA provision may include:

- º additional support to supplement the school's own SEN provision

- º placement in a special class or support centre at a mainstream school

- º placement in a special school

- º placement at a Pupil Referral Unit.

Fundamental to any school-based assessment and intervention/support programmes should be:

- º an understanding by all school staff of the cause and nature of AD/HD

- º agreed procedures for dealing with its manifestations

- º the fullest co-operation with the child's parents and understanding of the difficulties they are facing.

CHAPTER 8

Parents and the Assessment and Intervention Process

Parents are the foremost authorities about their own children. They may find it difficult to accept that their child is struggling and troublesome at school, but they do know if their child has academic problems and they are very aware of unacceptable behaviour. Parents will also have spent an enormous amount of time and energy in trying to find reasons for their child's problems so will probably be very knowledgeable about Attention Deficit / Hyperactivity Disorder. Probably the first and most important consideration that parents would like to be made, therefore is that time be taken to listen to them and act on what they have to say.

Parents often believe, and sometimes are made to believe by the very people they have approached for help and advice, that their child's behaviour is their fault. While AD/HD is not caused by bad parenting, it can make parents *look* and *feel* inadequate.

AD/HD can have a devastating effect on a family. Relationships within the family become strained and even break down in extreme cases. The parents may be unable to agree on the best way to deal with their child and blame each other overtly or covertly. This can cause the total breakdown of a marriage.

The mother usually takes the brunt of all the problems associated with this condition. Very often, she is the person who has to deal with the school, reactions from the extended family, friends and people out in the street, arrangements for assessments as well as the home management of the child with AD/HD.

Siblings may use the child with AD/HD as a 'spectator sport' by goading, teasing and daring. They may be jealous of the amount of attention given to their brother or sister and resent dispensations given for behaviour they themselves are not allowed to get away with.

Professor Martin Herbert, Consultant Clinical Psychologist at Exeter Clinical and Community Psychology Services, comments that people around AD/HD acquire 'learned helplessness', and this is very much in evidence in parents. Even when they have taken advice from other parents, friends, teachers and so on, they come to realise that nothing works for any extended period of time (Herbert 1996).

It is also extremely difficult for parents to describe what the problem is. All children evidence some of the behaviour seen in children with AD/HD from time to time, just not all at once, all day, every day!

Many parents are exhausted by the time a child is diagnosed as suffering from AD/HD. In some cases, they may have been battling for several years to find someone who can tell them why their child is so troublesome. They may feel they have been let down by the system and find it difficult to trust their own judgement and that of the professionals who are trying to help them. They may also feel angry, frustrated and resentful that it has taken so long to find solutions.

Parents need consideration, help and support when dealing with this condition. It is essential, therefore, that schools draw up guidelines to use when dealing with parents. Every effort must be made to keep communication between all concerned open, straightforward and honest. Awareness of the stresses and strains prevailing on parents of children with AD/HD must be taken into consideration. Parents question their own judgement when

AD/HD is an issue and therefore need someone they believe is 'on their side' and who is knowledgeable in this field.

There is a growing body of research to show that AD/HD is not only hereditary, but that many people carry features of this condition into adulthood. This means that many children with AD/HD may have one or more parents still suffering from various aspects of it, albeit with reduced severity. Home life can be chaotic and such families may just not be able to implement recommended strategies. Inappropriate social and communication skills may cause difficulties. Family counselling should be made available in these cases.

CHAPTER 9

Policy Guidelines

1. This book is based on recognition of the term AD/HD
    according to the criteria specified by the American
    Psychiatric Association in DSM-IV (see Appendix A).
    However, the diagnosis can be somewhat loosely applied
    and categorised, and rigour and careful consideration in the
    assessment and diagnostic process are very important.
    Independent reports should be obtained which provide
    valid, reliable data across at least two settings.

2. Ideally, medical diagnosis should have taken into account
    an accompanying psychological evaluation from either a
    clinical or an educational psychologist. There should be a
    psychological component to any intervention.
    Comorbidities with AD/HD should also be considered as
    part of the assessment and intervention process.

3. A psychological evaluation would essentially follow a
    problem-solving framework. A full cognitive assessment
    would not necessarily be implemented if observational data
    alongside evidence from the school did not implicate
    AD/HD type behaviours.

4. Effective intervention for children with AD/HD depends
    on cooperation between teachers, students and parents, and
    often the involvement of other professionals. The
    Individual Education Plan provides a good model for
    planning a response to AD/HD within the stages of the
    Code of Practice (see Chapter 7). Interventions should be

designed in terms of clear targets and definite strategies; they should involve parents and should have an evaluation component.

5. When working with parents and teachers to draw up an Individual Education Plan, issues of implementation, monitoring and evaluation need to be considered and agreed with parents, teachers, students and anyone involved in the programme. Collaborative working and shared information are the basis of all successful intervention programmes.

6. Among the group of children who are described as having AD/HD there is a wide spectrum of need stretching from those who may require minimal assistance at a particular point in their school career through to others who have complex and severe learning difficulties and who may need more intensive help. It is anticipated that most children with AD/HD will not go through all the stages as set out in the SEN Code of Practice. For the majority of pupils who have AD/HD, support should be forthcoming within a mainstream setting where they can have access to all aspects of the National Curriculum.

7. A diagnosis of AD/HD on its own is not grounds for automatic statutory assessment. Nevertheless, a diagnosis normally implies that the child should be on the SEN register.

8. Modification to classroom instruction and/or management is a powerful way to deal with students' attentional problems. Only after these issues have been addressed appropriately should other factors and/or interventions be investigated.

9. Teachers need to utilise appropriate instructional and behaviour management methods in order to educate students with AD/HD successfully. These competencies are

not separate from good teaching and should be integrated into total teaching practice. The principles of effective instructional and behavioural management procedures have been shown to provide a firm base of competencies for teachers working with children with AD/HD and behaviour disorders.

10. School policies need to be developed which support the school's endeavours with AD/HD and related problems. Teachers cannot be expected to deal with these problems in isolation.

11. In order for educators to deal effectively with students with AD/HD, there are many implications for training and development activities for teachers and school staff. Activities which may be required at the school level include development of:

    ° teachers' knowledge of specific instructional strategies for assisting a student with AD/HD

    ° teachers' knowledge of cognitive and behavioural strategies

    ° teachers' ability to programme for social skills training

    ° skills in collaborative consultation for working with other professionals, parents and care-givers.

12. While medication can be essential to a successful management/treatment programme it should not be used as a first measure or as the sole treatment in isolation to other management programmes. Medication should be prescribed in conjunction with other forms of intervention, such as psychological, social and educational, which help the child to develop skills, attitudes and behaviours that will enable them to cope with the demands of everyday life. Pills on their own are not a substitute for skills in the treatment of AD/HD.

13. The use of medication as an adjunct to behavioural management should only be on the recommendation of a doctor experienced in the management of children with AD/HD (i.e. consultant paediatrician or child psychiatrist) and requires ongoing supervision. It is recommended that medication should be prescribed as part of a shared care initiative with the child's general practitioner.

14. While psychologists and teachers need to contribute to the consultation process, ultimate decisions regarding medication should only be made by medical practitioners in consultation with parents and the child, and not by psychologists or teachers.

15. While there is no legal or contractual duty on school staff to administer medicine or supervise a pupil taking it (DfEE 1996, *Supporting Pupils with Medical Needs in School*) teachers and school staff have a common law duty to act as any reasonably prudent parent would to ensure the health and safety of their pupils. School staff should not, as a general rule, administer medication without first receiving appropriate information and/or training. This should be accompanied by a protocol from the medical practitioner giving clear instructions when they ask teachers to administer medication in school.

16. Not all children with a diagnosis will necessarily require or want medication. Conversely, medication for AD/HD is not always synonymous with a diagnosis of AD/HD. The effectiveness of the drug is not necessarily indicative of a diagnosis.

17. Medication should initially be prescribed on a trial basis only, with frequent monitoring of school performance and time spent off medication to re-assess behaviour and learning.

18. Communication between school professionals is critical to improve the evaluation of medication treatment. Medical practitioners should consult with education professionals in the collection of school evidence to aid in the objective assessment of medication. The medical practitioner should request and be provided with further information from school in order to monitor the effects of medication on the child's emotional, physical, cognitive and behavioural states.

19. Supervision of medication in a school setting needs to be discreet. *Many* children, particularly adolescents, do not want their friends to know, and may refuse medication due to peer pressure.

20. All those involved need to be aware of the concern that medication may be used as an expedient measure to provide the simplest and most instant results and can cover up symptoms implicating other causes.

21. There should be a clear school policy shared by staff, parents and pupils which provides a sound basis for ensuring that all pupils with medical needs receive proper care and support at school. Schools should not make selective judgements regarding the type of medication which is prescribed.

22. Parents benefit from having step-by-step guidelines on what to do. Such information should be clear, accessible and readily available and should include:

    ° whom parents should talk to first

    ° what questions to ask

    ° what information they will need to give to the school, their GP, the specialist and so forth

    ° guidelines for time taken and time limits for each stage of assessment towards diagnosis and treatment

    ° information about national and local support groups.

23. Many parents come to believe that information is being withheld at every stage. This increases their feelings of frustration and powerlessness. It is useful and beneficial to introduce a system whereby every agency, including the parents, could be provided with 'progress reports'. It is helpful if a form or questionnaire can be designed in such a way as to be quick and easy to complete and therefore quick and easy to issue.

24. Help may need to be made available from social services in assisting families who have a child with severe symptoms of AD/HD.

25. Communication among all professionals, including parents, should be regular, constructive and respect confidentiality and should have as its goal the care, well-being and long-term management of the child diagnosed as having AD/HD.

Diagnostic Criteria

DSM-IV Diagnostic Criteria for Attention-Deficit/Hyperactivity Disorder

A. Either (1) or (2)

(1) Six (or more) of the following symptoms of inattention have persisted for at least 6 months to a degree that is maladaptive and inconsistent with developmental level.

Inattention

a) Often fails to give close attention to details or makes careless mistakes in schoolwork, work, or other activities.

b) Often has difficulty sustaining attention in tasks or play activities.

c) Often does not seem to listen when spoken to directly.

d) Often does not follow through on instructions and fails to finish schoolwork, chores, or duties in the workplace (not due to oppositional behaviour or failure to understand instructions).

e) Often has difficulty organising tasks and activities.

f) Often avoids, dislikes or is reluctant to engage in tasks that require sustained mental effort (such as schoolwork or homework).

g) Often loses things necessary for tasks or activities (e.g. toys, school assignments, pencils, books or tools).

h) Is often easily distracted by extraneous stimuli.

i) Is often forgetful in daily activities.

(2) Six (or more) of the following symptoms of hyperactivity-impulsivity have persisted for at least 6 months to a degree that is maladaptive and inconsistent with developmental level:

Hyperactivity

a) Often fidgets with hands or feet or squirms in seat.

b) Leaves seat in classroom or in other situations in which remaining seated is expected.

c) Often runs about or climbs excessively in situations in which it is inappropriate (in adolescents or adults, may be limited to subjective feelings of restlessness).

d) Often has difficulty playing or engaging in leisure activities quietly.

e) Is often 'on the go' or often acts as if driven by a motor.

f) Often talks excessively.

Impulsivity

g) Often blurts out answers before questions have been completed.

h) Often has difficulty awaiting turn.

i)   Often interrupts or intrudes on others (eg. butts into conversations or games).

B.   Some hyperactive-impulsive or inattentive symptoms that caused impairment were present before age 7.

C.   Some impairment from the symptoms is present in two or more settings (e.g. at school [or work] and at home).

D.   There must be clear evidence of clinically significant impairment in social, academic or occupational functioning.

E.   The symptoms do not occur exclusively during the course of a Pervasive Developmental Disorder, Schizophrenia or other Psychotic Disorder and are not better accounted for by another mental disorder (e.g. Mood Disorder, Anxiety Disorder, Dissociative Disorder or a Personality Disorder).

ICD-10 Diagnostic Criteria for Hyperkinetic Syndrome

A. Demonstrate abnormality of attention and activity at home, for the age and developmental level of the child, as evidenced by at least three of the following attention problems:

1. Short duration to spontaneous activities.

2. Often leaving play activities unfinished.

3. Overfrequent changes between activities.

4. Undue lack of persistence at tasks set by adults.

5. Unduly high distractibility during study, (e.g. homework or reading assignment); and by at least two of the following.

6. Continuous motor restlessness (running, jumping, etc.).

7. Markedly excessive fidgeting or wriggling during spontaneous activities.

8. Markedly excessive activity in situations expecting relative stillness (e.g. mealtimes, travel, visiting, church).

9. Difficulty in remaining seated when required.

B. Demonstrate abnormality of attention and activity at school or nursery (if applicable), for the age and development level of the child, as evidenced by at least two of the following attention problems:

1. Undue lack of persistence at tasks.

2. Unduly high distractibility, i.e. often orienting towards extrinsic stimuli.

3. Overfrequent changes between activities when choice is allowed.

4. Excessively short duration of play activities, and by at least two of the following activity problems.

5. Continuous and excessive motor restlessness (running, jumping, etc.) in school.

6. Markedly excessive fidgeting and wriggling in structured situation.

7. Excessive levels of off-task activity during tasks.

8. Unduly often out of seat when required to be sitting.

C. Directly observed abnormality of attention or activity. This must be excessive for the child's age and development level. The evidence may be any of the following:

1. Direct observation of the criteria in A or B above, i.e. not solely the report of parent and/or teacher.

2. Observation of abnormal levels of motor activity, or off-task behaviour, or lack of persistence in activities, in a setting outside home or school (e.g. clinic or laboratory).

3. Significant impairment of performance on psychometric test of attention.

D.   Does not meet criteria for pervasive developmental disorder, mania, depressive or anxiety disorder.

E.   Onset before the age of six years.

F.   Duration of at least six months.

G.   IQ above 50. The research diagnosis of Hyperkinetic disorder requires the definite presence of abnormal levels of inattention and restlessness that are pervasive across situations and persistent over time, that can be demonstrated by direct observation, and that are not caused by other disorders such as autism or affective disorders. Eventually, assessment instruments should develop to the point where it is possible to take a quantitative cut-off score on reliable, valid, and standardised measures of hyperactive behaviour in the home and classroom, corresponding to the 95th percentile on both measures. Such criteria would then replace A and B above.

Physician's Checklist for Patients

Name:
Birthdate:
Current Age:
Sex: M __ F __
Date of evaluation:
Relationship:

Instructions: This checklist of questions should be reviewed periodically with parents of children taking stimulant drugs.

1. What dose have you been regularly giving to this child over the past month?
Medication:

Dose:

Have you noticed any of the following side effects this month?

☐ loss of appetite/weight

☐ insomnia

☐ irritability in late morning or late afternoon

☐ unusual crying

☐ tics or nervous habits

☐ headaches/stomach ache

☐ sadness

☐ rashes

☐ dizziness

☐ dark circles under eyes

☐ fearfulness

☐ social withdrawal

☐ drowsiness

☐ anxiety

3. If so, please describe how often and when the side effects occurred.

4. Have you spoken with the child's teacher lately? How is the child performing in class?

5. Did your child complain about taking the medication or avoid its use?

6. Has there been any change in your child's behaviour since last reviewed? If so, what seems to have changed?

7. Is the child's general health, growth (height and weight) and blood pressure satisfactory?

8. Have there been problems in giving the child medication at school?

Adapted from *Hyperactive Children: A Handbook for Diagnosis and Treatment* (1981) by R A Barkley, published by the Guilford Press, New York.

Follow-Up Information

Name:

Birthdate:

Current Age:

Sex: M ___ F ___

Medication administered (including dosage and frequency):

Indicate the frequency of the behaviours listed below, together with responses to medication:

BEHAVIOUR	FREQUENCY			MEDICATION EFFECTS		
Target symptoms	Never	Sometimes	Often	Improved	No change	Worse
Off task	☐	☐	☐	☐	☐	☐
Fails to finish work	☐	☐	☐	☐	☐	☐
Careless mistakes in work	☐	☐	☐	☐	☐	☐
Difficulty following instructions	☐	☐	☐	☐	☐	☐

BEHAVIOUR	FREQUENCY			MEDICATION EFFECTS		
Target symptoms	Never	Sometimes	Often	Improved	No change	Worse
Difficulty organising tasks/activities	☐	☐	☐	☐	☐	☐
Easily distracted	☐	☐	☐	☐	☐	☐
Restless and fidgety	☐	☐	☐	☐	☐	☐
Calls out excessively	☐	☐	☐	☐	☐	☐
Difficulty working with others	☐	☐	☐	☐	☐	☐
Aggressive	☐	☐	☐	☐	☐	☐
Fails to follow rules	☐	☐	☐	☐	☐	☐
Side effects						
Appetite loss	☐	☐	☐	☐	☐	☐
Insomnia	☐	☐	☐	☐	☐	☐
Weepiness	☐	☐	☐	☐	☐	☐
Irritability	☐	☐	☐	☐	☐	☐
Nervousness	☐	☐	☐	☐	☐	☐
Anxiety	☐	☐	☐	☐	☐	☐
Drowsiness	☐	☐	☐	☐	☐	☐
Sadness	☐	☐	☐	☐	☐	☐
Headaches	☐	☐	☐	☐	☐	☐

Any other comments:

Physical examination
Height:
Weight:
BP:
P:
Positive findings:

AD/HD Information Sheet for Parents

Suggestions for Keeping Your Child Safe

Most children with AD/HD experience more accidental poisonings and trips to hospital than do other children. There are several reasons why your child may be accident-prone:

- ° your child is impulsive and may do such things as running out into the street without looking

- ° your child seems to have no fear of, say, jumping off the porch roof for a dare

- ° the child may eat or drink something poisonous.

You need to be aware of what your child is up to at all times. Take steps to make your house and garden safe and childproof.

1. Watch your child closely when playing outside. Keep glass, rocks and other sharp items away from where your child plays. Secure rubbish bins. Ask neighbours to watch for your child as well.

2. Lock medicines, cleaning supplies, and other poisons where even the most determined child can't get them.

3. Cover all electrical outlets.

4. Put large, colourful stickers on sliding glass doors.

5. If you have a pool, make sure it is well fenced. Never leave your child unattended in the pool area.

6. Protect items you value. Put glass figurines, china, and jewellery out of reach.

7.   Firmly tie the cords of blinds or curtains. Do not allow them to hang loose.

8.   Store electrical appliances, knives, and tools in a locked cupboard away from areas where the child plays.

9.   Secure loose wires so your child can't trip on them.

10. Select toys that stand up to heavy use.

Always remember to compliment your child for playing safely: 'Well done! You know the right way to use the scissors!' Point out other children who are playing safely.

Taking Your Child Out to Public Places

1.   Think ahead to social situations that may be difficult. Will your child get bored or cause difficulty'?

2.   Before going into the situation...

   ° review your standing rules

   ° agree with your child on a reward for behaving well

   ° clearly state a consequence for non-compliance.

3.   Have your child restate the rule, consequence, and reward to make sure they are understood and remembered.

4.   Remind your child about the reward in a positive way while you are in the situation. Don't threaten the child. (That is to say 'If you remember..., you'll get to...' Not, 'If you don't behave right now, you won't get to...')

5.   Give the reward immediately on leaving the public place. Here's an example:

Anticipate: You have to take your child grocery shopping with you. You know your child has difficulty waiting in line at the cash register and grabs sweets.

Review the rule: 'When you are in line – hands to yourself. I'd like you to hold my purse while I pay.'

Determine a reward: You wanted to go to the duck pond. If you keep your hands to yourself, let's stop by the duck pond and feed the ducks'.

Review a consequence: 'If you take any sweets we won't see the ducks.' *Have the child restate:* 'Hands to myself. I can feed the ducks if I keep my hands to myself.'

Positively state reward as you shop: 'It's great to know we will be feeding the ducks!'

Reward your child immediately: Drive from the shop straight to the duck pond. State: 'When you follow the rules, nice things happen.'

6. If your child appears to be forgetting the rule, call attention to something else and positively state the reward again.

    Try this: 'Oh, look! There's a picture of a duck on that box. I wonder if we will see a duck like that?'

    Not this: 'You'd better behave or no ducks for you.

7. Avoid using the word 'Don't'. State something positive while you direct your child toward what you expect.

    Try this: 'I want to see your hands on the table.'

    Not this: 'Don't touch the plant!'

8. Keep your child involved. If your child will have to wait quietly, bring along something special to play with. Keep a box of small toys and books in your car just for this purpose.

9. Try to offer a balance between structured and unstructured activities. Remember, your child can do a formal 'sit-down' kind of activity for only a short time.

10. Learn to see trouble coming. When you see your child starting to lose control in a situation, step in right away. Offer a diversion that will help your child gain control. Do not encourage the overactive behaviour to continue.

11. Take care of yourself! At times, you may need to remove yourself from a difficult situation to cool off. Is there a friend or neighbour nearby you can call on short notice to take care of your child, even for only ten minutes'? Remind yourself of everything you are doing and the progress your child is making. Your efforts *will* make a difference.

References

Achenbach, T.M. (1991) *Manual for the Child Behaviour Checklist and Revised Child Behaviour Profile.* Burlington: University of Vermont, Department of Psychiatry.

American Academy of Child and Adolescent Psychiatry (1997) 'Practice parameters for the assessment and treatment of children, adolescents and adults with attention deficit / hyperactivity disorder.' *Journal of American Academy of Child and Adolescent Psychiatry 36, 10,* 855–1205.

American Psychiatric Association (1994) *Diagnostic and Statistical Manual of Mental Disorders, Fourth Edition, Washington, DC: American Psychiatric Press.*

August, G.J. (1987) 'Production deficiencies in free recall: A comparison of hyperactive, learning-disabled and normal children.' *Journal of Abnormal Child Psychology, 15,* 429–440.

Barkley, R. (1981) *Hyperactive Children: A Handbook for Diagnosis and Treatment.* New York: Guilford Press.

Barkley, R. (1991a) *Attention-Deficit Hyperactivity Disorder: A Clinical Workbook.* New York: Guilford Press.

Barkley, R. (1991b) 'The ecological validity of laboratory and analogue assessment methods of ADHD symptoms.' *Journal of Abnormal Child Psychology 19,* 149–178.

Barkley, R. (1995a) *Taking Charge of ADHD.* New York: Guilford Press.

Barkley, R. (1995b) 'Can neuropsychological tests help diagnose ADD/ADHD?' *The ADHD Report 2,* 1, 1–3.

Barkley, R. (1996) 'Attention Deficit Hyperactivity Disorder.' In E. J. Marsh and R. Barkley (eds) *Child Psychopathology.* New York: Guilford Press.

Barkley, R. (1997) *ADHD and the Nature of Self-Control.* New York: Guilford Press.

Barkley, R. (1998) *Attention Deficit Hyperactivity Disorder: A Handbook for Diagnosis and Treatment (2nd edition).* New York: Guilford Press.

Barkley, R., Dupaul, G.J. and McMurray, M.B. (1990) 'A comprehensive evaluation of attention deficit disorder with and without hyperactivity as defined by research criteria.' *Journal of Consulting and Clinical Psychology 58*, 775–789.

Biederman, J., Faraone, S.V., Doyle, A., Lehman, B. K., Kraus, I., Perrin, J. and Tsuang, M.T. (1993) 'Convergence of the Child Behaviour Checklist with structured interview-based psychiatric diagnosis of ADHD children with and without comorbidity.' *Journal of Child Psychology and Psychiatry 34*, 7, 1241–1251.

Borcherding, B., Thompson, K., Kruesi, M., Bartko, J., Rapoport, J. and Weingartner, H. (1988) 'Automatic and effortful processing in attention deficit / hyperactivity disorder.' *Journal of Abnormal Child Psychology 16*, 333–345.

Braswell, L. and Bloomquist, M.L. (1991) *Cognitive Behavioural Therapy with ADHD Children.* New York: Guilford Press.

British Psychological Society (1996) *Attention Deficit Hyperactivity Disorder (ADHD): A Psychological Response to an Evolving Concept.* Leicester: British Psychological Society.

Brown, T. E. (1997) *New Brown Attention-Deficit Disorder Scales (Brown ADD Scales).* New York: The Psychological Corporation.

Castellanos, F.X., Giedd, J.N., Marsh, W.L., Hamburger, S.D., Vaituzis, A.C., Dickstein, D.P., Sarfatti, S.E., Vauss, Y.C., Snell, J.W., Lange, N., Kaysen, D., Krain, A.L., Ritchie, G.F., Rajapakse, J.C., and Rapoport, J.L. (1996) 'Quantitative brain magnetic resonance imaging in Attention-Deficit Hyperactivity Disorder.' *Archives of General Psychiatry 53*, 607–616.

Cohen, M., Becker, M.G. and Campbell, R. (1990) 'Relationships among four methods of assessment of children with attention-deficit hyperactivity disorder.' *Journal of School Psychology 28*, 189–202.

Conners, C.K. (1997) *Conners' Rating Scales– Revised.* Toronto: Multi-Health Systems Inc.

Corkum, P. and Siegel, L. (1993) 'Is the continuous performance task a valuable research tool for use with children with Attention Deficit Hyperactivity Disorder?' *Journal of Child Psychology and Psychiatry 34*, 1217–1239.

Corkum, P. and Siegel, L. (1995) 'Debate and argument: Reply to Dr. Koelega: Is the continuous performance task useful in research with ADHD children? Comments on a review.' *Journal of Child Psychology and Psychiatry 36*, 8, 1487–1493.

Croll, P. (1986) *Systematic Classroom Observation.* London: The Falmer Press.

Department for Education (1994) *Code of Practice on the Identification and Assessment of Special Educational Needs.* London: HMSO.

Department for Education and Employment (DfEE) (1996) *Supporting Pupils With Medical Needs In School.* Circular 14/96. London: HMSO.

Du Paul, G. and Stoner, G. (1994) *ADHD in the Schools: Assessment and Intervention Strategies.* New York: Guilford Press.

Giedd, J.N., Snell, J.W., Lange, N., Rajapakse, J.C., Casey, B.J., Kozuch, P.L., Vaituzis, A.C., Vauss, Y.C., Hamburger, S.D., Kaysen, D., and Rapoport, J.L. (1996) 'Quantitative magnetic resonance imaging of human brain development: Ages 4–18.' *Cerebral Cortex, 6,* 551–560

Goldstein, S. (1995) *Understanding and Managing Children's Classroom Behaviour.* New York: John Wiley and Sons, Inc.

Goldstein, S. and Goldstein, M. (1995) 'Attention Deficit / Hyperactivity Disorder in adults.' *Directions in Psychiatry 15,* 18.

Goldstein, S. (1997) The First European Conference for Health & Education Professional on Attention Deficit / Hyperactivity Disorder: University of Oxford (unpublished manuscript).

Goodman, R. & Stevenson, J. (1989) 'A twin study of hyperactivity -II: The aetiological role of genes, family relationships and peri-natal adversity.' *Journal of Child Psychology and Psychiatry, 30,* (5), 691–709.

Hauser, P., Zametkin, A.J., Martinez, P. , Vitiello, B., Matochik, J.A., Mixon, A.J., and Weintraub, B.D. (1993) 'Attention-deficit hyperactivity disorder in people with generalised resistance to thyroid hormone.' *New England Journal of Medicine 328,* 997–1001.

Herbert, M. (1996) *Helping Hyperactive Children and their Carers: A Guide for Practitioners, Parents and Teachers.* Kenn, Devon: Impact Desktop Publications.

Hinshaw, S. (1992) 'Externalising behaviour problems and academic underachievement in childhood and adolescence: Causal

5555

5

relationships and underlying mechanisms.' *Psychological Bulletin,* *111,* 127-155.

Hinshaw, S. (1994) *Attention Deficit Disorders and Hyperactivity in Children.* Thousand Oaks, CA: Sage.

James, W. (1990) *Principles of Psychology.* London: Encyclopaedia Britannica. (Original work published 1890)

Kaufman, A.S. (1994) *Intelligent Testing with The WISC-III.* New York: John Wiley and Sons Inc.

Kendall, P.C. and Braswell, L. (1985) *Cognitive-Behavioural Therapy for Impulsive Children.* New York: Guilford Press.

Kewley, G. (1998) 'Personal paper: attention deficit hyperactivity disorder is underdiagnosed and undertreated in Britain.' *British Medical Journal 316;* 1594–6.

Koelega, H. S. (1995) 'Is the continuous performance task useful in research with ADHD children? Comments on a review.' *Journal of Child Psychology and Psychiatry 36,* 8, 1477–1485.

Palkes, H.S. and Stewart M.A. (1972) 'Intellectual ability and performance of hyperactive children.' *American Journal of Orthopsychiatry 42,* 35–39.

Pelham, W.F. and Milich, R. (1984) 'Peer relations of children with hyperactivity / attention deficit disorder.' *Journal of Learning Disabilities 17,* 560–568.

Prendergast, M., Taylor, E., Rapoport, J. L., Bartko, J., Donnelly, M., Zametkin, A., Ahearn, M. B., Dunn, G., and Wieselburg, H.M. (1988) 'The diagnosis of childhood hyperactivity – A US–UK cross-national study of DSM-III and ICD-9.' *Journal of Child Psychology and Psychiatry 29,* 289–300.

Richards, I. (1995) 'ADHD, ADD and dyslexia.' In P. Cooper and K. Ideus (eds.) *Attention-Deficit / Hyperactivity Disorder: Educational, Medical and Cultural Issues.* Maidstone, Kent: Association of Workers for Children with Emotional and Behavioural Difficulties.

Rosvold, H., E., Mirsky, A. F., Saranson, I., Bransome, E. D. and Beck, L.H. (1956) 'A continuous performance test of brain damage.' *Journal of Consulting Psychology, 20,* 343-352.

Schachar, R. (1991) 'Childhood hyperactivity.' *Journal of Child Psychology and Psychiatry 32,* 155–192.

Schwean, V. L. and Saklofske, D. H. (1998) 'WISC-III assessment of children with Attention Deficit/Hyperactivity Disorder.' In A. Prifitera and D. Saklofske (eds) *WISC-III: Clinical Use and Interpretation.* New York: Academic Press.

Sherman, D.K., McGue, M.K., and Iacono, W.G. (1997) 'Twin concordance for attention deficit hyperactivity disorder: A comparison of teachers' and mothers' reports.' *American Journal of Psychiatry 154,* 532–535.

Sonuga-Barke, E., Lamparelli, M., Stevenson, J., Thompson, M., and Henry, A. (1994) 'Behaviour problems and pre-school intellectual attainment: The associations of hyperactivity and conduct problems.' *Journal of Child Psychology and Psychiatry 35,* 949–960.

Sonuga-Barke, E. and Goldfoot, M. (1995) 'The effect of child hyperactivity on mothers' expectations for development.' *Child Care, Health and Development 21,* 1, 17–29.

Tannock, R. (1998) Attention deficit hyperactivity disorder: advances in cognitive, neurobiological, and genetic research. *Journal of Child Psychology and Psychiatry 29,* 289–300.

Tant, J.L. and Douglas, V. I. (1982) 'Problem-solving in hyperactive, normal and reading-disabled boys.' *Journal of Abnormal Child Psychology 39,* 1, 65–99.

Taylor, E. (1994a) 'Syndromes of attention deficit and overactivity.' In M. Rutter, E. Taylor and L. Hersov (eds) *Child and Adolescent Psychiatry: Modern Approaches (3rd edition).* Oxford: Blackwell Scientific Publications.

Taylor, E. (1994b) 'Hyperactivity as a special educational need.' *Therapeutic Care and Education (Special Issue on ADHD) 4,* 2, 130–144.

Taylor, E. (1995) 'Treating hyperkinetic disorders in childhood.' *British Medical Journal 310,* 1617–1618.

Taylor, E., Sandberg, S., Thorley, C. and Giles, S. (eds) (1991) *The Epidemiology Of Childhood Hyperactivity.* London: Oxford University Press.

Taylor, E. and Dowdney, L. (1998) 'The parenting and family functioning of children with hyperactivity.' *Journal of Child Psychology and Psychiatry 39,* 2, 161–169.

Ullman, R.K., Sleator, E.K. and Sprague, R.L. (1991) *Attention Comprehensive Teachers' Rating Scale: ACTeRS.* Illinois: MetriTech, Inc.

Van der Oord, E.J.C.G., Boomsma, D.I., and Verhulst, F.C. (1994) 'A study of problem behaviours in 10- to 15-year-old biologically related and unrelated international adoptees.' *Behaviour Genetics, 24,* 193–205.

Van der Oord, E.J.C.G., and Rowe, D.C. (1997) 'Continuity and change in children's social maladjustment: A developmental behaviour genetic study.' *Developmental Psychology 33,* 319–332.

Wechsler, D. (1992) *Wechsler Intelligence Scale for Children – Third UK Edition.* London: Harcourt Brace.

World Health Organization (1992) *The ICD-10 Classification of Mental & Behavioural Disorders, Clinical Descriptions and Diagnostic Guidelines.* Geneva: World Health Organization.

Zametkin, A.J., Nordahl, T., Gross, M., King, A.C. Semple, W.E., Rumsey, J., Hamburger, S. and Cohen, R.M. (1990) 'Cerebral glucose metabolism in adults with hyperactivity of childhood onset.' *New England Journal of Medicine 323,* 1351–1366.

Further Reading

For Parents

Barkley, R. (1995a) *Taking Charge of ADHD*. New York: Guilford Press.

Cooper, P. and Ideus, K. (eds.) (1995) *Attention Deficit/Hyperactivity Disorder: Educational, Medical and Cultural Issues*. Chariton Court, East Sutton, Near Maidstone, Kent: The Association of Workers for Children with Emotional and Behavioural Difficulties.

Fugitt, E. D. (1984) *'He Hit Me Back First!' Creative Visualisation Activities for Parenting and Teaching*. Jalmar Books.

Green, C. (1994) *Understanding ADD*. Doubleday. Australia.

Herbert, M. (1996) *Helping Hyperactive Children and their Carers: A Guide for Practitioners, Parents and Teachers*. Kenn, Devon: Impact Desktop Publications.

Kennedy, P., Terdal, L. and Fusetti, L. (1993) *The Hyperactive Child Book*. New York: St Martin's Press.

Lena, B. (1996) *Attention Deficit Disorder. ADHD. The Basics. What is it? What can you do about it?* Ottawa: Riverside Consultations Inc.

Nash, H (1994) *Kids, Families and Chaos. Living With Attention Deficit Disorder*. Torrensville, Australia: Ed.Med Publishers.

Nash, H (1994) *Medication for Attention Deficit Disorder*. Torrensville, Australia: Ed.Med Publishers.

Serfontein, G. (1990) *The Hidden Handicap. How to help children who suffer from Dyslexia, Hyperactivity and Learning Difficulties*. New York: Simon and Schuster.

Serfontein, G. (1994) *ADD in Adults*. Torrensville, Australia: Simon and Schuster.

Taylor, J.F. (1994) *Helping Your Hyperactive/Attention Deficit Child*. Rocklin: Prima Publishing.

Train, A. (1996) *AD/HD: How to Deal with Very Difficult Children*. London: Souvenir Press.

For Children

Quinn, P. O. and Stern, J. M. (1991) *Putting on the Brakes. Young People's Guide to Understanding Attention Deficit Hyperactivity Disorder (ADHD)*. New York: Magination Press.

Quinn, P. O. and Stern, J. M. (1993) *The 'Putting on the Brakes' Activity Book for Young People with ADHD*. New York: Magination Press.

For Adults

Cooper, P. and Ideus, K. (eds) (1995) *Attention-Deficit / Hyperactivity Disorder: Educational, Medical and Cultural Issues*. Maidstone, Kent: Association of Workers for Children with Emotional and Behavioural Difficulties.

Cooper, P. and Ideus, K. (1996) *Attention Deficit / Hyperactivity Disorder: A Practical Guide for Teachers*. London: David Fulton Publishers.

Dowling, E. and Osborne, E. (1994) *The Family and The School: A Joint Systems Approach to Probelms with Children (2nd Ed)*. London: Routledge.

Goldstein, S. and Goldstein, M. (1992) *Hyperactivity: Why Won't My Child Pay Attention?* New York: John Wiley and Sons, Inc.

Hallowell, E.M. and Ratey, J. (1996) *Attention Deficit Disorder*. London: Fourth Estate Limited.

Kelly, K. and Ramundo, P. (1993) *You Mean I'm Not Lazy, Stupid or Crazy?! A Self-Help Book for Adults with Attention Deficit Disorder*. London: Simon and Schuster.

Solden, S. (1995) *Women with Attention Deficit Disorder. Embracing Disorganization at Home and in the Workplace*. Grass Valley: Underwood Books.

Taylor, E. (1985) *The Hyperactive Child*. London: Dunitz.

This is by no means a comprehensive list of books available on the subject of Attention Deficit / Hyperactivity Disorder. The books listed have been acquired from various different sources which are listed below:

Local Library

Your library may not have all of these books on their shelves but they can order them from other libraries in your county. They will probably charge for this service.

Local Bookshop

Please note that some bookshops do have a range of books on this subject while others will do their best to order them on request.

Mail Order

The ADD/ADHD Family Support Group UK
Mrs B Tuffill
93 Avon Road
Devizes SN10 1PT
Tel: 01380 726710

LADDER
National Learning and Attention Deficit Disorders Association
PO Box 700
Wolverhampton WV3 7YY
Tel: enquiries 01902 336272; members and fax 01902 336232

ADD Information Services
PO Box 340
Edgware HA8 9HL
Tel: 0181 905 2013
Fax: 0181 386 6466

Further Information
and Contact Addresses

Support Groups, Assessment and Resource Centres
National

The AD/HD Family Support Group UK
1a High Street
Dilton Marsh
Westbury
Wiltshire BA 13 4DL
Tel: Mrs Gill Mead 01373 826045

ADD Information Services
PO Box 340
Edgware HA8 9HL
Tel: 0181 905 2013
Fax: 0181 386 6466

ADDNet UK
10 Troughton Road
Charlton
London SE7 7QH
Tel/fax: 0181 305 1023

Contact A Family
170 Tottenham Court Road
London W1P 0HA
Tel: 0171 3833555

Department for Education and Employment (DfEE)
Elizabeth House
York Road
London SE1 7PH
Code of Practice SEN
Tel: 0171 510 0150

The Hyperactive Children's Support Group
71 Whyke Lane
Chichester
West Sussex
Tel: Sally Bunday 01803 725182

IPSEA Legal Advice for SEN
Tel: 01394 382814

Network 81
Advice on Special Educational Needs
Tel: 01279 503244

LADDER
National Learning and Attention Deficit Disorders Asscociation
142 Mostyn Road
London SW19 3LR
Tel: 0181 543 2800
Fax: 0181 543 4800
or
95 Church Road
Bradmore
Wolverhampton WV3 7EW
Tel: enquiries 01902 336272; members and fax 01902 336232

The Learning Assessment Centre
2nd Floor
44 Springfield Road
Horsham
West Sussex RH12 2PD

Tel: Pauline Latham (Practice Manager) 01403 240002
Fax: 01403 260900

International Children and Adults With Attention Deficit Disorders
(CHADD)
1859 North Pine Island Road
Suite 185
Plantation,
FL 33322
USA
Tel: (001) 305 587 3700

University of Massachusetts Medical Centre
Attention Deficit Hyperactivity Disorder Clinic Department of
Psychiatry
University of Massachusetts
55 Lake Avenue North Worcester,
MA 01655-0239
USA
Tel: (001) 508 8956 2552
Fax: (001) 508 856 3595

AD/HD Websites
www.web-tv.co.uk/addnet.html
ADDNet UK home page. Premier AD/HD-related UK site on
the web.

www.chadd.org
Children and Adults with Attention Deficit Disorder –
'CHADD'. US website which is probably the largest support
group/information network on AD/HD in the world.

www.pavilion.co.uk/add/english.html
European AD/HD home page.

www.pncl.co.uk/~prosper/adhd.html
Information about the ADD/ADHD Family Support Group.

www.patient.org.uk
UK self-help and patient group web links.

www.azstarnet.com/~ask
Website for adults seeking knowledge about AD/HD.

www.psychinfo.org
UK conferences on AD/HD and medical information from
International Psychology Services (IPS).

ww.ncet.org.uk/senco SENCO
Information exchange from The National Council for
Educational Technology Resources for Special Needs.

www.add.org
US home page for ADDA (the more adult-oriented AD/HD
support group).

www.shef.ac.uk/~psyc/InterPsych/inter.html
Very useful mental health resource with numerous powerful
features.

www.mediconsult.com/frames/add
One of the best medical information sites on the web.

www.aacap.org
The home page for the American Academy of Child and
Adolescent Psychiatry presents a 'fact sheet' about AD/HD in
several languages and also a library of research abstracts from
recent scientific meetings.

Subject Index

accident proneness 18
Achenbach rating
   scales 25–26
ACTeRS (Attention
   Comprehensive
   Teachers' Rating
   Scale) 26
addiction 54
adolescence 21–22
adulthood 22
affective disorders 76
age-appropriate
   behaviour 15, 28
American Academy of
   Child and
   Adolescent
   Psychiatry 29
American Psychiatric
   Association 65
antecedents, recording
   of 36
anxiety disorder 18,
   20, 23, 73, 76
syndrome 20
assessment
   clinical and medical
      examination
      30–31
   integrating data
      31–32
   psychological
      27–30
   school performance
      27

associated disorders
   18
asthma 30
attention abnormality,
   evidence of 75–76
attention problems
   listed
   home environment
      74
   school environment
      74–75
attentional capacity 28
attentional deficit
   disorder (ADD) 13
autism 20, 23, 76

background outline to
   AD/HD 13–14
Barkley Home and
   School Situations
   Questionnaires 26
behaviour across
   settings 23,
   25–26
behavioural influences
   19
behavioural inhibition
   disorder (BID) 14
bioenvironmental
   influences 22
biological factors,
   influence of 16,
   22
book's objectives 12

categorical clinical
   decision-making
   19
causes of AD/HD
   15–17, 22

central nervous
   system infection
   30
cerebral-vascular
   disease 30
characteristics of
   AD/HD 14
classroom
   observation 26
clinical examination
   30–31
clinically significant
   zone 19
clumsiness 17
cognitive
   deficits 20
   processes 19
   profile 27–30
collaborative
   approach 12,
   52, 66 see also
   multi-
   disciplinary
   approach
combined type
   AD/HD 24
communication 49,
   69, 70
communication,
   practical hints
   49
   17–18, 30, 65
conflict resolution
   37
confrontation and
   conflict 50
Conners' rating
   scales 26
consistency see
   routine

Continuous Performance Test (CPT) 28–29

control, parental 49–50

creativity, special talents 48

daily routines *see* structured daily routines

definition of AD/HD 14–15

depression 20

developmental history 25, 30 shifts in symptoms 21–22

Diagnostic and Statistical Manual of Mental Disorders, 1998 (American Psychiatric Association) 73

diagnostic complexity 15, 18–20, 24 criteria for AD/HD 23, 71–73 criteria for Hyperkinetic Syndrome 74–76

differential diagnosis 18, 30

disability perspective 42, 46

disorder 73

dopamine 15

DSM-IV Diagnostic Criteria 18, 65, 71–73

duration of symptoms 23

dyslexia 18

early school years 21

ecological validity in diagnosis 29

educational provision evidence for statement of special needs 58–59 evidence for statutory assessment 58 fundamentals for assessment and support 59 LEA support and placement for those with special needs 59 National Curriculum, access to 58, 66 Special Educational Needs, Code of Practice 57 specialist advice recommended 58

emotional temperature reduction 50–52

enuresis 18

environmental considerations 15, 19 factors, influence of 16, 22

processes 19

epilepsy 30

etiligy (aetiology) *see* causes

evaluation components 24, 26

evidence for statement of special needs 58–59 for statutory assessment 58 of symptoms 23

Exeter Clinical and Community Psychology Services 62

expectations 50

family assistance 70 history 25, 30 relationships 61

feedback 46

follow-up 55, 80–82

networks 16

genetic basis for neurodysfunction in AD/HD 16

group work 37–38

head trauma 30

health problems 18

hearing deficit 30

hemisphere dysfunction 16

Herbert, Professor Martin 62

hereditary nature of
AD/HD 63
high blood pressure
30
home intervention
see also school
intervention
advice and
collaboration 52
communication 49
control 49–50
emotional
temperature
reduction 50–52
expectation, realism
in 50
ignoring, planned, as
sanction 51
knowledge and
understanding,
development of
46
overview 45
positive thought and
action 46–47
routine, structure and
predictability 48
self-esteem 47–48
stress and respite 52
time-out as sanction
51–52
home liason 41–42
homework diaries 35
*Hyperactive Children: A
Handbook for
Diagnosis and
Treatment*, 1981
(Barkley, R.A.) 79

hyperactive-impulsive
(predominantly)
type AD/HD 24
hyperactivity,
symptoms of 72
hyperkinetic syndrome,
diagnostic criteria
for 74–76
hypoxia 30

ICD-10 Diagnostic
Criteria 74–76
impulsivity, symptoms
of 72–73
inattention, symptoms
of 71–72
inattentive
(predominantly)
type AD/HD 14,
24
incidence rate
discrepancies *see*
prevelance
independent reports,
need for 65
Individual Educational
Plan 65, 66
infancy 21
information sheet for
parents 83–86
integrating assessment
data 31–32
intellectual
development 17
*International
Classification of
Diseases*, 1990
(World Health
Organization) 76
intervention

at home 45–52
at school 33–43
strategy 15,
65–66

James, William 13

learning
behaviour 28
difficulties 17, 18,
20, 29

mania 76
medical examination
34–31
medical treatment for
AD/HD 15, 31,
53–55
medication
addiction 54
as adjunct to
behavioural
management
67–68
decision to treat
55
expediency in use
69
follow-up 55
ineffective aspects
of methyl-
phenidate use
53
not necessarily
required 68
overview 53–54
primacy of medical
practitioner in
decision-
making 68
side effects 54

and treatment
    53–55
trial basis initially
    68
(Ritalin) 13, 53–54
minimal brain
    dysfunction 13
mood disorder 23, 73
mother's role 61–62
motivational support
    35
multi-dimensional
    conceptualisation
    16–17, 19–20, 24
multi-disciplinary
    approach 34, 55
    see also collaborative
    approach
multi-modal assessment
    and treatment 20,
    24, 33
multiple sampling 19

National Curriculum
    58, 66
need, spectrum of 66
neurotransmitters 15,
    54
noise levels 36
    15

objectives of this book
    12
onset of symptoms 23
outings to public
    places, suggestions
    for coping 84–86
overrepresentation of
    boys see
    prevalence

parent-therapist
    collaboration 52
parental
    exhaustion 62
    feelings of
    inadequacy 61
    guidelines 69–70
    involvement 70
    need for support
    62–63
    role 66
    understanding 46
parents
    as authorities on
    their children 61
    difficulties in
    describing the
    problem, 62
    proposed
    information sheet
    for 83–86
partial remission 24
patients
    physician's checklist
    for 77–79
    physician's follow-up
    data form 80–82
peer group support 37
performance
    anxiety 29
    difficulties 39
personality disorder
    23, 73
pervasive
    developmental
    disorder 73, 76
pharmacological
    intervention see
    medication
physician's

checklist for
    patients 77–79
    follow–up 80–82
positive
    attention 46–47
    attributes, focus
    upon 39–40
    behaviour,
    reinforcement
    of 36
    outcomes, focus
    upon 35
predictability see
    routine
preschool years 21
prevalence 11, 21
psychological
    evaluation
    27–30, 65
Psychology, Principles
    of (James,
    William) 13
psychosis 23, 73
public places,
    suggestions for
    coping with
    outings to
    84–86
punishment 46

quiet areas 35

rating scales
    behaviour across
    settings 25–26
    subjective nature
    26 see also
    Achenbach;
    Conners;
    ACTeRS;
    Barkley

re-engagement 35
recording work, range
    of ways 40
research evidence on
    causes inconclusive
    15
rewards, primary and
    secondary 46
routine, structure,
    predictability 34,
    48

safety suggestions
    83–84
sanctions 36, 50–52
schizophrenia 23, 73
school intervention
    see also home
    intervention
    clarity in policy 69
    classroom
        organisation
        34–35
    discreetness in
        supervision of
        medication 69
    fundamentals for
        assessment and
        support 59
    home liason 41–42
    individual needs
        39–41
    lesson presentation
        35–36
    managing behaviours
        36–37
    overview 33–34
    physical
        arrangements 35
    social skills 37–38

summary of
    strategies 42–43
teaching style
    38–39
utilisation of
    appropriate
    management
    methods 66–67
school records review
    26–27
self-esteem 18, 39,
    47–48
serotonin 15
sibling rivalries 62
sleeping patterns 18
social competence
    17–18, 37–38
Special Educational
    Needs (SEN), Code
    of Practice on the
    Identification and
    Assessment of 57,
    65, 66
statutory assessment
    66
Still, George 13
stress and respite 52
structured daily
    routines 34
Supporting Pupils with
    Medical Needs in
    School, 1996
    (DfEE) 68
symptoms of AD/HD
    20, 21–22

targets and rules
    36–37
task conditions 29
teacher's role 66–68

teacher training 67
teaching
    considerations
    see school
    intervention
teaching style
    38–39
Tourette's syndrome
    20, 30

underdiagnosis and
    treatment in
    Britain see
    prevalence

viral encephalitis 13
visual deficit 30

Intelligence Scale
    28, 29

Author Index

Achenbach, T.M. 25-26
American Academy of Child and Adolescent Psychiatry 29
American Psychiatric Association 73
August, G.J. 28

Barkley, R. 14, 17-19, 26, 28, 29-30, 79
Barkley, R., Dupaul, G.J. and McMurray, M.B. 29
Biederman, J., Faraone, S.V., Doyle, A., Lehman, B.K., Kraus, I., Perrin, J. and Tsuang, M.T. 26
Borcherding, B., Thompson, K., Kruesi, M., Bartko, J., Rapoport, J. and Weingartner, H. 28
Braswell, L. and Bloomquist, M.L. 28
British Psychological Society 12, 16
Brown, T.E. 26

Castellanos, F.X., Giedd, J.N., Marsh, W.L., Hamburger, S.D., Vaituzis, A.C., Dickstein, D.P., Sarfatti, S.E., Vauss, Y.C., Snell, J.W., Lange, N., Kaysen, D., Krain, A.L., Ritchie, G.F., Rajapakse, J.C. and Rapoport, J.L. 16
Cohen, M., Becker, M.G. and Campbell, R. 29
Conners, C.K. 26
Corkum, P. and Siegel, L. 28
Croll, P. 26

Du Paul, G. and Stoner, G. 17, 29, 31

Education, Department for 27, 57
Education and Employment, Department for (DfEE) 68

Giedd, J.N., Snell, J.W., Lange, N., Rajapakase, J.C., Casey, B.J., Kozuch, P.L., Vaituzis, A.C., Vauss, Y.C., Hamburger, S.D., Kaysen, D. and Rapoport, J.L. 16
Goldstein, S. 18, 26

Goldstein, S. and Goldstein, M. 55
Goodman, R. and Stevenson, J. 16

Hauser, P., Zametkin, A.J., Martinez, P., Vitiello, B., Matochik, J.A., Mixon, A.J. and Weintraub, B.D. 16
Herbert, M. 62
Hinshaw, S. 11, 17

James, W. 13

Kaufman, A.S. 28
Kendall, P.C. and Braswell, L. 16
Kewley, G. 11
Koelega, H.S. 28

Palkes, H.S. and Stewart, M.A. 17
Pelham, W.F. and Milich, R. 17-18
Prendergast, M., Taylor, E., Rapoport, J.L., Bartko, J., Donnelly, M., Zametkjn, A., Ahearn, M.B., Dunn, G. and Wieselburg, H.M. 11

Richards, I. 17
Rosvold, H.E., Mirsky,
    A.F., Saranson, I.,
    Bransome, E.D. and
    Beck, L.H. 28

Schachar, R. 11
Schwean, V.L. and
    Saklofske, D.H. 28
Sherman, D.K., McGue,
    M.K. and Iacono,
    W.G. 16
Sonuga-Barke, E., and
    Goldfoot, M. 16
Sonuga-Barke, E.,
    Lamparelli, M.,
    Stevenson, J.,
    Thompson, M. and
    Henry, A. 17

Tannock, R. 11, 17,
    29
Tant, J.L. and Douglas,
    V.I. 28
Taylor, E. 11, 29
Taylor, E. and
    Dowdney, L. 16
Taylor, E., Sandberg, S.,
    Thorley, C. and
    Giles, S. 11

Ullman, R.K., Sleator,
    E.K. and Sprague,
    R.L. 26

Van der Oord, E.J.C.G.,
    Boomsma, D.I. and
    Verhulst, F.C. 16
Van der Oord, E.J.C.G.
    and Rowe, D.C.
    16

Wechsler, D. 28
World Health
    Organization 76

Zametkin, A.J.,
    Nordahl, T., Gross,
    M., King, A.C.,
    Semple, W.E.,
    Rumsey, J.,
    Hamburger, S. and
    Cohen, R.M. 16

Also published by Jessica Kingsley Publishers

Asperger's Syndrome
A Guide for Parents and Professionals

Tony Attwood

240 pages ISBN 1 85302 577 1 pb
Despite having been defined over fifty years ago, until the last few years very few people had heard of Asperger's Syndrome. Yet since the syndrome has become more widely known and more frequently diagnosed parents and professionals have found themselves increasingly in need of authoritative information and guidance.

In this comprehensive work, the first of its kind, Tony Attwood has created a guide that will assist parents and professionals with the identification and treatment of both children and adults with Asperger's Syndrome. The book provides a description and analysis of the unusual characteristics of the syndrome and practical strategies to reduce those that are most conspicuous or debilitating. Beginning with a chapter on diagnosis; including an assessment test, the book covers all aspects of the syndrome from language to social behaviour and motor clumsiness, concluding with a chapter based on the questions most frequently asked by those who come into contact with individuals with this syndrome.

This guide brings together the most relevant and useful information on Asperger's Syndrome, based on an overview of the available literature and incorporates case studies, from the author's own practical experience as a Clinical Psychologist, with examples of, and numerous quotations from people with Asperger's Syndrome.

Tony Attwood is a practising Clinical Psychologist who specialises in the field of Asperger's Syndrome. For the last twenty-five years he has met and worked with several hundred individuals with this syndrome, ranging widely in age, ability and background.

Also published by Jessica Kingsley Publishers

Understanding and Supporting Children with Emotional and Behavioural Difficulties

Edited by Paul Cooper

250 pages ISBN 1 85302 666 2 pb
ISBN 1 85302 665 4 hb

Children with emotional and behavioural difficulties (EBDs) present a challenge for parents, teachers and other professionals alike. *Understanding and Supporting Children with Emotional and Behavioural Difficulties* is a comprehensive guide to this group of ill-defined, often unrelated disorders, which can cause children to become disruptive both at school and in the home. It examines the nature of EBDs and their potential causes, whether social, psychological or biological, and discusses the issues that can arise for professionals involved in their assessment, describing and analysing the various methods used.

The contributors stress that EBDs are ultimately a form of communication, albeit an antagonistic one, and evaluate the success of different methods of intervention in clinical, educational and family settings. They argue that successful intervention in any environment requires an appreciation of the complex interplay in the social and personal factors affecting each child. Finally the book explores the future of EBDs and their treatment, calling for a greater understanding of children with EBDs and improved cooperation between the educational and medical forms of intervention.

Paul Cooper is Lecturer in Education in the School of Education, University of Cambridge.

Also published by Jessica Kingsley Publishers

From Thoughts to Obsessions
Obsessive Compulsive Disorder in
Children and Adolescents

Per Hove Thomsen

pages ISBN 1 85302 721 9 pb

Obsessive compulsive disorder (OCD) is the term given to a condition characterized by recurring obsessive thoughts or actions. These thoughts or actions are involuntary and are often a response to a deep-rooted but irrational fear. This introductory book, richly illustrated with case examples, explains the nature and treatment of OCD in children and adolescents. OCD has been little discussed in relation to this age group, although it is now believed that approximately 1 per cent of all children and adolescents suffers from serious obsessive disorders.

Written for parents and relatives as well as doctors, teachers and other professionals working with this group of patients, *From Thoughts to Obsessions* defines OCD and forms a straightforward explanation of the symptoms, assessment procedures and treatment strategies. Per Hove Thomsen also examines obsessive features which may form part of normal adolescent development as well as the relationship of OCD to other psychiatric conditions.

Per Hove Thomsen is a specialist in child psychiatry who has, for a number of years, worked with the research and treatment of obsessive behaviour in children and adolescents. He is Head of the Research Centre at the Child and Adolescent Psychiatric Hospital in Århus, Denmark.

Also published by Jessica Kingsley Publishers

Children with Autism, 2nd edition
Diagnosis and Intervention to Meet Their Needs

Colwyn Trevarthen, Kenneth Aitken,
Despina Papoudi and Jacqueline Robarts

368 pages ISBN 1 85302 555 0 pb

This completely revised and substantially expanded new edition embraces new developments in this rapidly developing field. Every chapter has been rewritten with the addition of new material, and a new final chapter on 'Putting the Pieces Together' reflects the authors' conviction that the complexity of autism means that many kinds of information are valuable and need to be taken into account in providing therapy or teaching for children with autism.

Other chapters, updated from the first edition, include a description of the latest information on the findings of brain research (put into the context of the development of the human brain and its effect on communication in early childhood), and the contributions of music therapy and psychoanalysis. A very much enlarged chapter on educational provision for children with autism and Asperger's Syndrome provides information on the latest methods for improving the learning of these children, to give them the best possible preparation for a life of greater autonomy and maximum self-satisfaction in the pleasure of human company. New appendices summarise medical diagnostic systems, checklists and questionnaires for identifying autism, and the glossary has been considerably expanded. The wealth of up-to-date information provided will be invaluable not only for researchers and students but also for psychologists, teachers and other professionals, and parents, carers and family members in search of comprehensive and helpful information.

Colwyn Trevarthen is Professor of Child Psychology and Psychobiology at Edinburgh University. **Kenneth Aitken** is Principal Clinical Neuropsychologist at the Royal Hospital for Sick Children, Edinburgh. **Despina Papoudi** is Candidate Assistant Professor in Special Education, Department of Primary Education at the University of the Aegean, Rhodes. **Jacqueline Robarts** is Research Fellow in Music Therapy, City University London and Senior Music Therapist and Clinical Tutor at the Nordoff-Robbins Music Therapy Centre, London.